PENSIONS AND SURVIVAL

THE COMING CRISIS OF MONEY AND RETIREMENT

By Geoffrey N. Calvert

a Financial Post book

Maclean-Hunter Limited

ISBN 0-88896-057-3

Printed and bound in Canada

Contents

Introduction

This book is a basic review of the outlook for pensions in Canada, a discussion of the demographic and economic trends with which pensions are inseparably linked, and an analysis of certain proposals for change.

It covers not only the vast public pension systems, such as Old Age Security and the Canada and Quebec Pension Plan (C/QPP), but also the separate plans which have been established for employees both of the federal and provincial governments and also of private employers, large and small, and the self-employed.

It looks at the present and the future, and what the future holds both for pensioners and for taxpayers and others who will have to provide pensions in the years ahead.

It probes such questions as the emerging ratio of pensioners to workers, capital formation, the indexing of pensions, the funding of the C/QPP and of the provincial pension systems, the cash and other needs of the elderly, the changes needed in private pension plans, and the best age for retirement.

It looks at the situation not only from the viewpoint of the present generation of workers and pensioners, but also from the viewpoint of our children who will be expected to make good on the promises and commitments that we make now.

1

This book's approach is to get down to first principles and to present solutions which appear logical and in the best long-term interests of the Canadian people, regardless of present practices or vested interests. The author has tried to call the shots as they are, without fear and without any influence.

There are many weaknesses in the present approach to pensions, both public and private, and there are certain trends in the pension system which are now in the process of gradually undermining the Canadian economy. The author has attempted to show how improvements can be made which will strengthen Canada's position and reverse or eliminate these adverse trends.

This is a book for all the people of Canada, for the young as well as the old, for the legislator, the businessman, and the union leader, for the actuary, the trustee and plan administrator, as well as for the pension plan member and the self-employed worker. It is a book for women as well as for men, and for the mobile worker who changes his job often as well as the career employee. Unavoidably, it presents some technical material, but the aim has been to make it *readable* as well as thought-provoking and informative.

The preparation of this book was undertaken at the request of a group of employers*, most of them represented in the Canadian Pension Conference, who felt that a fundamental pension study was needed. The work was done under the aegis of the Canadian Pension Conference, with the knowledge of the federal government and with much assistance from its several departments involved in some way with pension and related statistics, and with the ready help also of many other organizations, both governmental, semi-governmental and private, too numerous to list. While all of these co-operated marvelously in the provision of data and assistance, here gratefully acknowledged, the author alone has developed the analysis and conclusions shown herein.

*Among them: The Canadian Pension Conference; Aluminum Company of Canada Ltd.; Bank of Montreal; Canada Packers Limited; Canadian Industries Limited; Canadian National Railways; Domtar Limited; Dupont of Canada Limited; Elliott & Page Limited; Inco Limited; Morguard Trust Company; Noranda Mines Limited; The Royal Trust Company; Saskatchewan Wheat Pool; Shell Canada Limited; The Steel Company of Canada; Sun Life Assurance Company of Canada; Tomenson-Alexander Limited; Wood Gundy Limited.

No one else is responsible in any way for the observations or judgments herein. Huge volumes of data, reports, speeches, computer runs, surveys, books and articles went into its preparation. The assembly and digestion of all of this material took approximately eight months ending in June 1976.

It is hoped that this work will provide fresh insights and much ground for discussion, and will thus lead to a deeper understanding and the development of sound policy in the field of pensions in Canada.

Geoffrey N. Calvert
Sidney, B.C.
August 29, 1976

3

CHAPTER ONE

The Tidal Wave

The sweeps of time

Pension fund work is long-term work. At each point of time, one looks far enough into the future to see through to the end of the life of each person now at work.

To most of us, the next century seems remote. But three quarters of those living in Canada today will still be here when the next century arrives, and 40% will celebrate a birthday in the year 2025. Less than half of those at work now, and none of those at school, will have reached retirement age when the next century arrives. The great majority of us will not retire in this century, but in the next century. The realities of that period are indeed of great concern to us.

Fortunately, there are ways of looking into the future. Demographic projections can be made, for example, which indicate one important dimension of the shape of things to come. There are uncertainties. No one can be sure of the future vagaries and caprices of the birth rate. But there are some very strong general trends. Immigration, too, is hazardous to predict. But it is certain that the pressure from outside to enter Canada will tend to increase, and the net inflow will thus reflect government policy. Death rates and expectations of life change very slowly. So, if we

4

are not trying to look more than 50 or 55 years into the future, we can be fairly sure about the numbers of people who will be living in Canada at ages above 60 or 65 at the end of that time, because they have already been born and are at school or at work. Only variations in the immigration factor can upset the projection, and changes from that source are not likely to be too severe because the number of immigrants will not likely be too great in relation to the number of Canadians who are already here.

It is with this sense of time, then, that we have to look at the commitments that are now being made and proposed for the provision of pensions and comfortable living standards for all Canadians, including those who will not retire for several decades.

The provision of these pensions will, of course, be a direct charge against, or allocation from, the gross national product of the future. If the size of the work force is large and the retired segment of the population is small, the burden of carrying these pensions will be light. If the work force shrinks and the retired population swells, the burden will become heavy, all other things being equal.

One has to be disturbed, then, to note the presence of a fundamental threat to the integrity of the entire system of pensions and old age benefits in Canada—a factor which even now is cutting away the base from under the whole system, even though it does not in any way affect the benefit levels presently enacted into law. What this factor does do, however, is to take lethal aim at the capacity of the working population to support the older sections of the population. With a cold inevitability, it compounds the upward cost pressures already built into the system through indexing and earlier retirement, or earlier pension commencement dates. This factor is the birth rate.

The Canadian birth rate

Birth rates are extremely sensitive to economic, political and environmental changes. Exactly nine months after the evacuation of the British army at Dunkirk, for example, the birth rate in the United States shot up like a skyrocket. This was not so much a manifestation of sympathy or excitement as a sense of the impending involvement of America in war, and a deep instinct for

5

survival. In the long depression years of the 1930s, with their heavy unemployment and economic hardships, birth rates had been very low, leaving as their legacy a thin stratum of population now in the early-to-mid-40s. But once World War II had started, the birth rate sharply reversed its long downtrend, and in the exuberant years after the war had ended it reached heights not seen since the early 1920s. Medical advances had by this time all but eliminated infant deaths, reinforcing the power of these high birth rates to cause a quickening population growth. The demographic legacy of this period of optimistic and enthusiastic building for the future has been a surge of young people sweeping up through the schools and colleges who now are entering the work force and are in the early years of family formation. These young people will be reaching retirement age in the decade beginning about the year 2015.

By the year 1960, something seemed to have changed deep down in the Canadian consciousness and indeed in that of the western world. The murderous street gangs in which the youth of the 1950s had sought protection and survival had given place to the hippies and flower children, the commune dwellers and pot smokers. The young people of the 1960s were rejecting and opting out of the world of materialism and of the tedium of commuting daily from suburbia which was supposed to have been the breeding ground of social contentment. Retired from the work force before the age of 20, these young people were telling us something very deep about our civilization.

But there was another silent messenger, perhaps telling us the same thing but in a different language, a sign language that few had learned to read. The birth rate had started to go down. Throughout most of the 1960s it fell headlong with a gathering acceleration, pausing only briefly at the end of the decade before sinking again lower. There was a pause in the area just south of the Canadian border exactly nine months after that November 1965 night of the sudden blackout—the widespread and prolonged failure of electric power, triggered in Canada by the failure of a small piece of equipment—which gave New York a ghoulish, freakish night, never to be forgotten by those who experienced it. A great city was prostrate in total darkness, blanketed by an eerie sense of impending doom. For once there was practically no crime at all,

6

though the opportunities were unparalleled; there was every-where a sense of extreme crisis and immediate catastrophe, and conceptions of babies occurred at many times the normal rate. Perhaps it was that deep basic instinct for national survival at work again.

Many causes have been cited for the long fall in the birth rate, among them:

1. The surge of women into the paid work force, felt by many to be incompatible with the bearing and raising of children.

2. Widespread use of the Pill, the Intra-Uterine Device and vasectomies.

3. Distribution of contraceptives through welfare agencies.

4. Dire warnings about the worldwide population explosion and a changed attitude about family size.

5. Legalized abortions, which may by now be numbering about one third of the number of live births.

Despite these developments, one cannot escape the feeling that the declining birth rate (in many parts of the western world it has penetrated below the zero-population-growth level and shows every sign of staying down there) reflects a deep concern, buried away somewhere in the inner psyche of the nation, perhaps a fa-talism about the future, a lack of that instinctive determination to continue the race and to build or continue our present way of life. It is something to be concerned about, and since it impinges di-rectly on the underpinnings of our whole system of pensions, our hopes and dreams of retirement, it is entirely relevant to this study.

There is a critical number in all this that should be watched. This is the total number of births per 1,000 females through their whole lives. If this figure is 2,098 or more, the population will just sustain itself or will grow in the long run. If it is less over a long period, the population will fail to reproduce itself, and, in the ab-sence of immigration, it will:

First, shrink in size.

Second, get older, on average.

Then eventually cease to exist.

The 2,098 total fertility rate corresponds at present with a "crude birth rate" of about 16.2 per 1,000 each year in the popu-lation as a whole.

So what are the recent facts in Canada?

Compared with a 16.2 crude birth rate needed just to stay even, these have been the actual rates:

1970	17.5			
1971		16.8		
1972			15.9	
1973				15.5
1974					15.4

As the demographic surge of our present young people have begun to have their own babies, there was in 1975 a very slight reversal to a figure of 15.7, still well below 16.2. This merely masks with a temporary statistical camouflage the continuing fall in the total fertility rate, which has cascaded down through the key figure of 2,098 as follows:

1970	2,331			
1971		2,187		
1972			2,024	
1973				1,931
1974					1,875

When the official long-term projections of benefit outflows, tax inflows and tax rates necessary to sustain the Canada Pension Plan (CPP) in future years were being prepared in Ottawa some time ago, these last figures were not available, and a total fertility rate of 2,159 was used as the basis of projection.

There is a 13% difference between 2,159 and 1,875, which is the last observed rate in what seems to be a continuing decline. Even if the rate were now to stabilize at 1,875, there would in due course be a 13% shrinkage in the work force available to support the pensioner population, and before long that would again compound into the second generation, as the spiral of demographic shrinkage continued and the nation became older and went into a decline. Only an increased flow of immigration could slow the trend.

In all the warnings about overpopulation and resource depletion, no attention seems to have been paid to what zero population growth means in terms of the youthfulness or aging of the population—the capacity of society to maintain its elderly sections

8

in the degree of comfort to which they have become accustomed. Perhaps the youth and vigor of the population is itself a resource which is now being deliberately curtailed in the interest of protecting other resources, and in time this will extract its own price. It is one thing to have a population that does not grow. It is quite another to have a population that burdens its work force with a higher and higher proportion of the elderly.

The special position of Quebec

Long recognized as the province with the highest birth rates and largest families, Quebec is now leading Canada in this headlong descent to lower birth rates. It was in the early 1960s that Quebec's birth rates first fell behind the Canadian average. By 1967 the difference had become substantial. More recent figures indicate a continuing substantial gap. (In Europe, it is West Germany that has similarly led the way to very low fertility levels.) The tables below and overleaf will be of interest, indicating among other things that the tax rates needed to support the Quebec Pension Plan (QPP) and the CPP may not always be able to run parallel. Note, too, that Quebec's lower net immigration rate does nothing to offset the disturbing effects of these differences.

Crude birth rates (per 1,000 of population)

	Quebec	All Canada
Average 1921-25	35.5	27.4
1926-30	30.5	24.1
1931-35	26.6	21.6
1936-40	24.6	20.7
1950	30.0	27.1
1955	29.5	28.2
1960	26.8	26.8
1965	21.2	21.3
1967	17.3	18.2
1970	15.3	17.5
1971	14.8	16.8
1972	13.8	15.9
1973	13.8	15.5
1974	14.0	15.4

Total fertility rates (number of births per 1,000 females)

	Quebec	All Canada
1960	3,764	3,895
1966	2,646	2,812
1972	1,727	2,024
1974	1,657	1,875

Do these birth rates have something to tell us? Do they simply reflect a more depressed economy, which may in time be corrected, or is there something else deeply burdening the inner psyche of the people of Quebec?

Today it is the northwestern frontier, the province of Alberta, the Yukon and the Northwest Territories, with their atmosphere of challenge and anticipation, that stand at the other extreme of Canada's birth rates. We must not try to read more from these figures than there is in them, but if there is something there, we should be alert to sense what it is.

Chart I, opposite, shows the recent history of the crude birth rate in Canada as a whole (the solid line). After a long secular fall in the birth rate, continuing through many decades (not all included in the chart), this chart shows that:

1. The birth rate had reached a level of about 28 per 1,000 in 1922.

2. Throughout the 1920s (which were not depressed) and continuing into the deeply depressed 1930s, it fell by a full 25% to 21 per 1,000.

3. With the outbreak of war, it surged back strongly to more than 28 per 1,000, remaining high for almost 20 years. (At the same time under the influence of the new antibiotics, infant death rates and childhood diseases were brought largely under control, making these high birth rates doubly effective in causing a vast increase in the numbers of children surviving to adult ages. It is the survivors of these children who comprise the human tidal wave now entering the work force, and who in due course will enter their retirement years.)

4. The new steeply falling trend which had first appeared even before the beginning of the 1960s has continued ever since, even after a loss of almost one half of the former rates.

10

CHART I

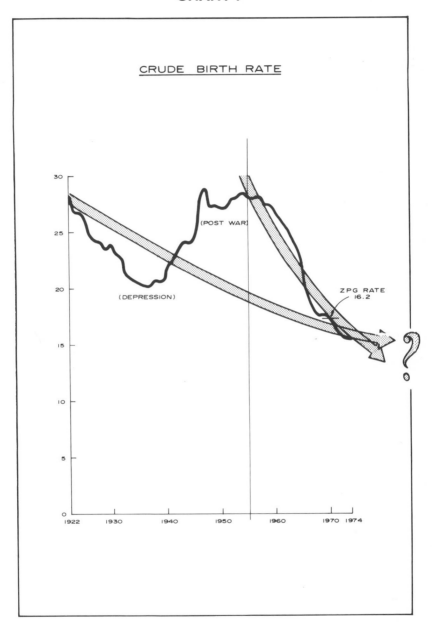

CRUDE BIRTH RATE

(POST WAR)

(DEPRESSION)

ZPG RATE
16.2

CHART II

Immigration To and Emigration From Canada, 1946-1986

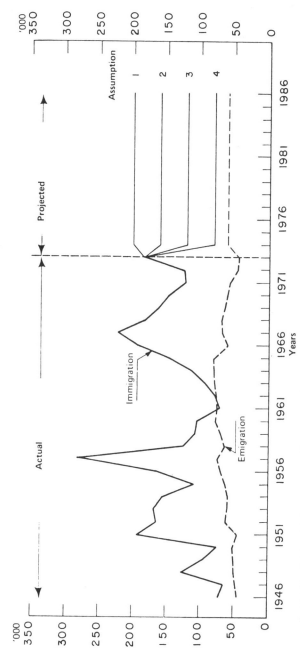

Sources: Immigrants — Canada, Department of Manpower and Immigration. Immigration Statistics, 1946 to 1972. Immigration Division, DMI, Ottawa.
Emigrants — Estimates prepared in the Population Estimates and Projections Division, Statistics Canada, Ottawa.

5. As the swollen cohorts of children born in the fertile 1950s begin to reach child bearing age, there seems to be a slight and weak reversal (though this is not supported by the continued downtrend of the underlying total fertility rate).

Where will the birth rate go from here? This question has serious implications for everyone in Canada. Economists, stock analysts, pension fund managers and labor negotiators are continually speculating and arguing about the future of the stock market, the consumer price index, the index of productivity, the general level of wages or the Canadian dollar. All these are important to the design and funding of pension plans; but many of these professionals are inclined to yawn and gaze out the window when the question of the birth rate comes up. Actually, this factor has a more fateful long-term impact than any of those mentioned. Quite apart from its supremely human and broad social aspects, it is an economic force of great sensitivity and overwhelming strategic power.

For the purpose of our present projections, we have assumed that the fertility rate, having fallen thus far, will fall no further, but will stabilize itself at its last recorded level of 1,875. There is no doubt that reality will turn out to be different, but no one can say how different, or when or in which direction the rate will change. Seemingly convincing arguments can be put forward both for a recovery and for a further decline. We shall assume neither. We shall, however, assume that immigration will continue to flow into Canada in a sufficient volume to bring about a continued, though slow, growth.

The rate of immigration

Chart II, opposite, adapted with permission from the book of population projections published by Statistics Canada (Catalogue 91-514), shows the volatile past history of immigration and emigration.

While emigration has not varied widely, immigration has been most erratic. In making some of its projections, Statistics Canada used a *net* immigration rate of 60,000 annually. This assumes 120,000 in and 60,000 out each year (line three and the dotted line in the chart).

For our present projections, and in view of the continued fall in the birth rate, we have stepped up this net immigration rate to 85,000, based on 145,000 in and 60,000 out each year. On the chart, this is a little above half-way between lines two and three, which seems to be a fair assumption.

In this matter, our projection basis is again less rosy than that used by the Department of Insurance in Ottawa, which assumes a net immigration rate of 113,000 in 1975, increasing steadily to 163,000 in 2000 and 210,000 in 2025. This basis was probably arrived at when Canada's immigration policy was temporarily much more liberal than it has since become. It may be that pressures from Third World countries with bursting populations could eventually force a higher Canadian immigration rate. But the sad truth is that even a tenfold increase in Canadian immigration starting now would make no noticeable difference at all to the problems of those Third World countries.

It is always easy to be wise with the benefit of a few extra years of hindsight. The question that cannot help but come up now is whether Ottawa's basis of the official CPP cost and tax projections, with its high birth and immigration rate assumptions, may not have turned out to be too optimistic, and hence tend to underestimate the tax rates needed to support the benefits inherent in the plan. It is our opinion that this is probably the case.

Population pyramids

The population pyramid is to the demographer what binoculars are to the field commander—his means of seeing things that are far away. At the base of the pyramid are shown the numbers of very young children, aged 0-4 years, males at the left and females at the right. The next layer shows those aged 5-9, and successive layers show successively higher age groups. A pyramid with a wide base and a thin top portrays a young population with many children and few old people. A pyramid with a cut-in base reflects a fallen birth rate. A pyramid with a heavy-looking top and a small base shows an aging population.

As time passes, each layer or "cohort" moves slowly up the pyramid, so the shape at any one time foreshadows the future shape. The birth rate, combined with the size of the child-bearing

CHART III

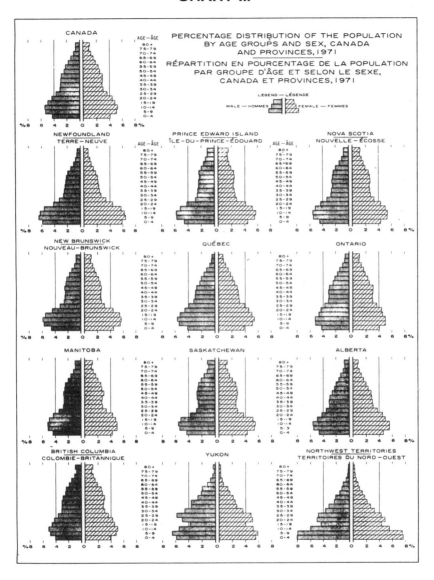

PERCENTAGE DISTRIBUTION OF THE POPULATION
BY AGE GROUPS AND SEX, CANADA
AND PROVINCES, 1971

RÉPARTITION EN POURCENTAGE DE LA POPULATION
PAR GROUPE D'ÂGE ET SELON LE SEXE,
CANADA ET PROVINCES, 1971

LEGEND — LÉGENDE

MALE — HOMMES   FEMALE — FEMMES

15

cohorts, determines the size of each new bottom layer. Pronounced bumps or hollows along the ascending slopes of a pyramid are the legacy of past periods of high or low birth rates, war casualties or unusual migration. As time goes by, these irregularities will work their way inexorably up the pyramid.

Chart III, on page 15, prepared and published by Statistics Canada on the basis of the 1971 census (Catalogue 92-715), shows the pyramids not only for Canada but also for each province.

Note for example:

—The cutting away at the base of all but one of these pyramids, which had already started well before the 1971 census.

—The abnormal age distribution of the Saskatchewan population, with a high proportion of older people and youths but an unusually slim mid-section in the prime work-force ages.

—The youthfulness of those in the Northwest Territories— very few old people but many children.

—The general similarity of the Quebec, Ontario and all-Canada pyramids in 1971. If the differences in birth and immigration rates, noted earlier, continue into the future, this similarity will not long continue.

Turning to the future, we see in Chart IV a graphic delineation of the outlook for the Canadian population, based on our assumption of a continuation of the recent birth and somewhat increased immigration rates described earlier. In this chart, which contains one of the basic messages in this book, one can watch the tidal wave of today's young people entering the work force, sweeping up through it, and then entering the retirement ages, radically changing the whole balance between young and old, and between workers and pensioners at each stage of their forward' surge through the age groups.

With these radical increases in the ratio of pensioners to workers clearly before us, it would seem to be unwise for Canada to commit itself to vast and liberal programs of support for its older people if these would result only in an overbalancing and collapse of the economy of the future. At least the matter should be further explored. Nor should we look only to the end of this century, when today's young people will be in the prime of their working careers and not yet ready for retirement. It is to the early part of the next century that we must look, when these same young

CHART IV

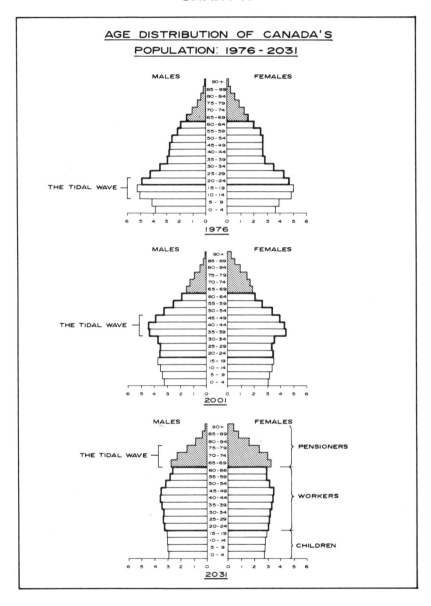

AGE DISTRIBUTION OF CANADA'S
POPULATION: 1976 - 2031

people, who are all with us today, will be approaching and entering their retirement years. It is in that period, a good deal less than 50 years from now, that the real consequences of decisions made today will begin to become all too apparent, and most of us here today will be present to see it.

The source of our concern about these charts does not stem only from the swollen cohorts of population now entering the work force, but equally from the shrunken cohorts that will follow them up through the age groups. It is this shrunken generation, also with us today and as yet unborn, that will have to carry the burden of pensions for their more numerous parents and elders, and to face the prospect of tax burdens that would almost certainly be rejected in short order by today's voters.

It is the abrupt sequence of larger-then-smaller generations that carries within it the seeds of real trouble for the future of all non-funded pension systems. Had the birth rate stayed above 20 or 21 per 1,000, with a fertility rate of, say, 2.6 babies per woman, this impending pension strain would not arise. The next generation of workers would be more ample, and the pension burden per worker less onerous. But the situation portrayed in these charts has already developed and continues to develop further with a compelling inevitability. One is reminded of Omar Khayyam's lines:

"The moving finger writes; and having writ,
Moves on: nor all thy piety nor wit
Shall lure it back to cancel half a line . . ."

We cannot look at the future as though nothing had changed. There are very fundamental forces at work.

For the next few decades, our judgment of relative pension costs can very easily be thrown off by the consequences of the earlier economic disorders of the 1930s. The generation that *preceded* the post-World War II surge, which occupies the middle range in today's work force, is a shrunken generation, born in those depressed years. The retirement of this generation will have commenced well before the close of the present century, at which time the work force will still be occupied by the ample cohorts of their immediate successors. Short-term (such as 25-year) projections of pension costs will thus be influenced to falsely show that the pension burden which lies ahead is light enough and easily carried.

18

But like a rising tide, the real surge of costs will envelop those who will pay their taxes a little later.

Since programs and policies adopted now cannot easily be retracted once they have commenced, it is to this somewhat later period that we must look in examining the feasibility of what is now proposed.

The population pyramids in Chart IV are helpful, too, in enabling us to visualize the effects of a change in retirement age. Thus if most people are retiring today at about age 65, and if this were abruptly changed to 60, the effect would be to remove the age 60-65 cohort from the work force and include it in the retired population. The resulting shock to the economy and the further pension strains that would follow can be seen in Chart V, overleaf, which shows the impact of universal retirement at age 60 on the pensioner-to-worker ratio, and the worsening outlook for this ratio in the future.

The ratio of retirement-age to work-age populations

Later in this book we shall examine the basic question of whether the practice of retirement at a fixed age, as it is accepted today, really makes sense. But for the present we shall assume that there will be no change in this practice, and that all of those who reach the fixed age will in fact retire and become dependent on others. The questions now to be examined are these:

1. What is the future outlook for the ratio of the retired to the active workers? This is a measure of the "pension burden" to be carried by the economy and society.

2. What would be the effects of dropping the retirement age from 65 to 60, or to 55 as has been done by the federal government for its civil servants, if these became universal practices?

From the projections which underlie Chart IV, we have calculated the ratios of population above age 65 to population aged 20 to 65 at each point in the future. These ratios are:

For 1976.............. 15.60%
2001.............. 18.41%
2031.............. 33.37%

CHART V

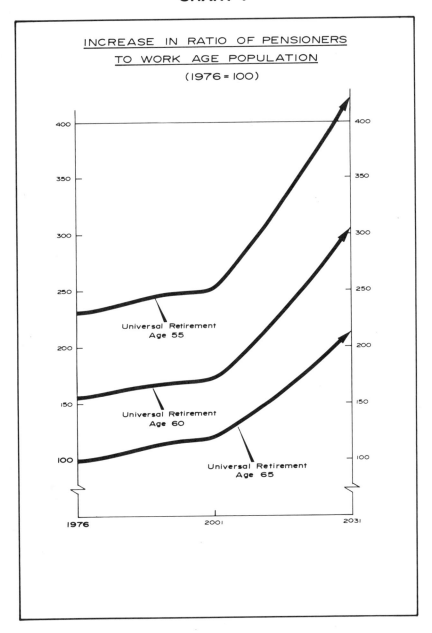

INCREASE IN RATIO OF PENSIONERS
TO WORK AGE POPULATION
(1976 = 100)

Universal Retirement
Age 55

Universal Retirement
Age 60

Universal Retirement
Age 65

1976   2001   2031

Note the acceleration after the year 2000, and note also that the ratio in 2031 will be *more than double* what it is today, so that even if there were no increase in the average income of the retired section in relation to the working section, the pension burden would more than double. In fact, as the CPP matures and many of the private plans also mature, the relative income of the average retired person will almost certainly increase, and the share of the gross national product going to the retired section would therefore seem likely to increase by well over 100%. The basic cause of this increase is demographic and inescapable.

Now let us see what happens when the retirement age is lowered from 65 to 60. This table shows the effects:

		Ratio	
Year	**Retirement at:**	**Age 65**	**Age 60**
1976		15.60%	24.41%
2001		18.41%	26.65%
2031		33.37%	47.66%

It may seem a bit staggering, but it is nevertheless true that a lowering of the retirement age from 65 to 60 would cause an immediate shift of more than 50% in the ratio of retired to working-age people. Further, in combination with the inexorable demographic process now at work, this ratio would *triple* before the end of the working lifetimes of those now at school in Canada. This is indeed a sobering fact.

But let us not stop there. There are already pension plans in operation that provide a 30-and-out retirement rule, and there are various government pension plans, such as the federal government plan referred to, which enable an eligible employee to retire on the full accrued and indexed pension at age 55. What, then, would become of these ratios if all citizens were to follow the example so clearly provided by their government? This table provides the answers:

		Ratio		
Year	**Retirement at:**	**Age 65**	**Age 60**	**Age 55**
1976		15.60%	24.41%	36.10%
2001		18.41%	26.65%	38.96%
2031		33.37%	47.66%	65.84%

Instead of a doubling of the pension burden per worker in coming decades, or a tripling of it if retirement were at age 60, this step, combined with the demographic change in progress, would *more than double the pension load at once and more than quadruple it* by the year 2031. Would Canada's economy be able to survive without a breakdown under the load of two pensioners for every three workers? Is this the direction in which the government should be leading us?

In this era, there are indexes for nearly everything. We have wage indexes and consumer price indexes and stock market indexes and temperature-humidity indexes and many others. As soon as something has to be lived with over a long period and watched carefully as it changes through time, somebody thinks of indexing it. Once it has its index, it becomes much more respectable and important and widely noticed and understood. Nobody in his right mind would think of doing something that would quadruple the consumer price index or the temperature-humidity index. It occurs to us that governments should be watching another index that does not exist yet, but maybe it should. This would be the Transfer Payment Index, and it would measure the percentage of the GNP going into all pension and welfare benefits that are not funded but are paid out of current taxation. In countries such as Britain and Italy, the index would be very high, and the problems of their ailing economies could be diagnosed with reference to this along with the index of days lost through strikes, and their inflation (CPI) indexes, and all the others. One of the sub-indexes entering into this basic Transfer Payment Index would be the Pension Cost Index, and once it is set in motion, future governments would ignore it at their peril. It is something the economy will have to cope with just as it has to cope with the balance of payments or the rate of inflation or the national debt.

If we start from the present by assigning a value of 100 to the Pension Cost Index in 1976, and ignore all influences at work other than the retirement age and the demographic changes described earlier, the outlook for the index appears in the table at the top of the opposite page.

Even if the benefit levels under pension plans are not increased relative to wages in the next 55 years, and retirement ages are not lowered at all, the work force in 2031 will have more than

Year	Retirement at:	Pension Cost Index		
		Age 65	**Age 60**	**Age 55**
1976		100.0	156.5	231.4
2001		118.0	170.8	249.7
2031		213.9	305.5	422.1

twice as heavy a pension burden to shoulder as that of 1976. If the trend to earlier retirement continues, the burden may increase to three or even four times the 1976 cost.

There are of course some other factors at work, such as the effects of the temporary partial funding of the CPP, the maturing of the CPP, and the interplay between this and the various income support and supplementation systems that exist in Canada, and future changes in the participation rate of women and men in the labor force. But in its own rough and ready way, this table shows the big picture.

Does it not conjure up strong feelings about the direction in which this whole pension and retirement movement is nudging the economy? Will such a pension system in the end turn out not only to be self-destructive, but also destructive of its host economy? Or will those born after World War II find that their dream of golden years in retirement somehow, like a rainbow, always moves on ahead of them and eludes them in the end, because they are too many, and their children are too few?

Can the dependency ratio help?

There are some who will point out that, as the pensioner load grows, the burden of raising children is getting less due to the falling birth rate, so that the *total* burden of pensioners-plus-children may not increase very much, and we therefore have nothing very important to be concerned about.

If we were simply playing a game of statistics, this argument would seem quite specious. However, it overlooks these fundamentals:

1. We are dealing with *people*, not figures.

2. Apart from land, labor and capital, productivity depends on *motivation*.

3. There is a world of difference between (a) going out to work

23

to earn money to feed, clothe and educate one's own children—a basic drive that occurs right through nature, and is not limited to man—and (b) going out to work to earn money only to have it taxed right out of your pocket.

It makes no difference to the worker how the tax money is applied. Whether it goes to pay pensions to elderly persons unknown, or paperwork and salaries of civil servants, or to buy battleships or monuments, it is still a tax, and it destroys the reward and the incentive to work. Caring for and paying for one's own children has the *very opposite* effect on most parents.

4. With the advance in technology, the movement of the work force into the servicing industries, and the knowledge explosion, it is necessary for young people to spend longer in school and university than in former times, and to enter the work force later. This is a continuing trend which largely cancels out, and may even more than cancel out, the effect of the shrinkage in the ratio of children to workers.

5. In any case, the *timing* of the argument is off by a whole generation. Those now in the work force and about to enter it are enjoying and will enjoy *both* the economic "advantages" of a not-too-onerous pension load *and* a shrunken generation of children, and will set their consumption patterns accordingly. *It is their children*, above all others, who will have to withstand the shock of vastly increased taxes for pensioners.

Only a pedant, of shallow understanding in this field, could ever look for relief in the dependency ratio.

CHART VI

TOTAL POPULATION AND ACTIVE WORK FORCE
(Males: 1971)

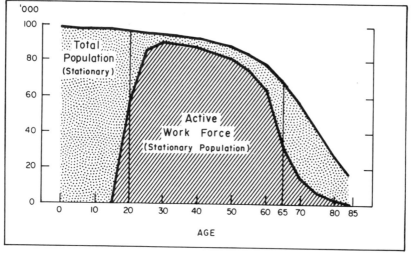

Other aspects of the demographic picture

Before leaving these demographic aspects of Canada's outlook for pensions, we present the following interesting and important aspects of the subject. Charts VI-IX are taken from the Working Life Tables issued by Statistics Canada in December 1975 (Catalogue 71-524F), and Charts X and XI from material furnished to us by the office of the Minister of Health and Welfare.

Chart VI, above, shows the age profile of the male population and male work force, calculated on a "stationary population" basis, that is, as though the rates of birth, death and immigration had remained steady over a long period. While it is evident that entry into and exit from the work force are spread over several years on either side of ages 20 and 65, the use of the entire population between these ages gives a reasonable approximation to the size of the work force. It is regrettable that no similar chart is available for the female population.

CHART VII

AVERAGE YEARS OF
FUTURE WORK AND RETIREMENT
(Males: 1971)

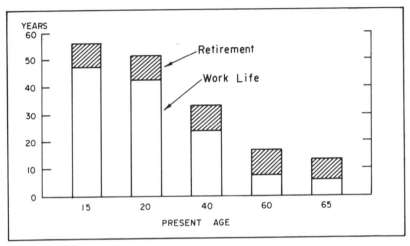

Chart VII may be helpful in visualizing the relative expectations of future work life and retired life, as now seen by an individual at various ages ranging from 15 to 65, under the conditions existing in 1971. To those above age 60, the whole subject of pensions and life in retirement lies immediately ahead and dominates everything else, while the outlook for the next century is of little more than academic interest. To those now in the 15-20 year age group, who are far more numerous, 40 or 50 years will pass before retirement age is reached. These are the members of the population who are or should be very much concerned with the next century, and with the rates of taxation they will have to face before they retire, and whether pension promises made now will perhaps wither in their hands before they, too, retire.

26

CHART VIII

LATER ENTRY INTO WORK FORCE
(Men: 1931-1971)

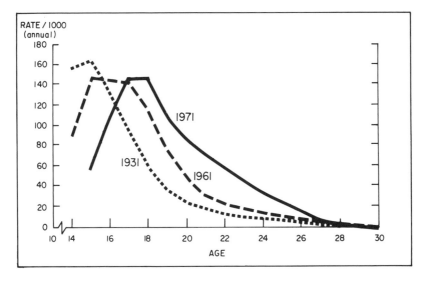

Chart VIII shows how, over the years, male workers have been entering the work force later and later as the shift from farm to factory and the rise in technology and the knowledge explosion have required longer and longer periods of education.

This continued deferment of entry into the work force, which may continue, has not been taken into account in calculating the ratios of retired to working populations. So far as these ratios and indexes are concerned, it is a factor which adds to the problem, tending to shrink the work force but not the retired population.

CHART IX

EARLIER EXIT FROM WORK FORCE
(Men: 1931-1971)

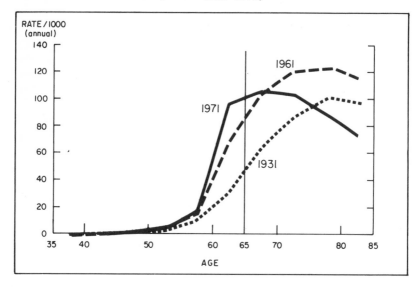

Chart IX shows three curves reflecting annual rates of exit from the work force observed respectively in 1931, 1961 and 1971. That for 1931 reflects the conditions that existed before pension plans came into general use. By 1961 many pension plans had been established and there was a modest government old age pension at age 70. Men were moving out of the work force earlier. By 1971, the CPP had come into being, but had not yet built up very significant pensions, while both the private plans and the old age pension had been extended and improved. The exodus from the work force had moved to a still lower average age. We have already seen what this continued movement to an earlier retirement age portends by expanding the retired population at the expense of the active work force.

28

Women to the rescue

While men have been entering the work force later and leaving it earlier, women have been surging into the work force. Between 1956 and 1973 there was this movement:

Women 14 years of age and over:	1956	1973
In school	4%	10%
In the home	65%	47%
Working or seeking work	25%	39%

By 1975 the participation rate of women had further increased to 41% and was continuing to grow. The 3,623,000 women (including 2,027,000 married women) at work or seeking work in June 1975 constituted about 35% of the total Canadian labor force.

Charts X and XI, overleaf, show how women in every age group have participated in this movement, and how the fall in the birth rate has coincided in time, in every age group, with this movement into the work force.

This migration of women from the home to paid employment is significant from a pension point of view in two ways:

1. Many are now earning CPP and private pensions in their own right and are less dependent on their husbands' pensions or survivor benefits.

2. Their work and taxes contribute to the GNP and to the support of those currently drawing non-funded pensions, helping to neutralize the later entry and earlier exit of men.

CHART X

PARTICIPATION RATE OF WOMEN BY AGE GROUP

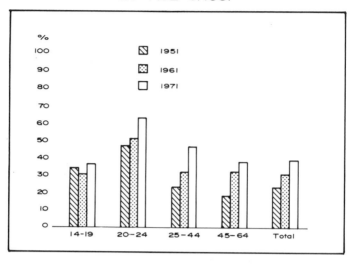

CHART XI

BIRTHS PER 1000 WOMEN BY AGE GROUP

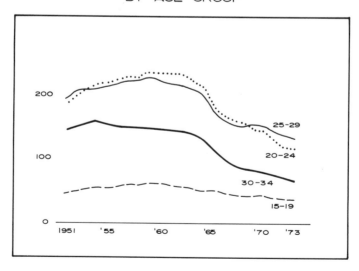

30

Fewer hours, more capital

In studying the capacity of the Canadian economy to provide for an increasing proportion of pensioners, it is not sufficient to look only at the ratio of pensioners to workers. One has also to consider the *hours worked* by these workers, and their *productivity*, which is related to the amount of *capital employed*.

A shrinking trend in average hours worked per worker is clearly mirrored in the following figures from Labor Canada. These relate to production-line workers in manufacturing:

	Normal Working Hours	Holidays per Year	Vacation Weeks Per Year	Net Work Week*	Index
1947	45.3	4.2	2.2	43.0	100.00
1951	43.5	6.2	2.4	40.7	94.7
1957	41.6	7.3	2.5	38.6	89.8
1961	41.3	7.5	2.7	38.1	88.6
1966	41.0	8.0	2.9	37.5	87.2
1972	40.4	9.1	3.3	36.5	84.9

(*Adjusted for vacation and holiday time)

In *25 years* there had been a *15% shrinkage* in the hours actually worked per member of the work force. *If this trend continues, while at the same time the GNP is to grow, and the growing proportion of pensioners is to be provided for, the onus shifts heavily to the other major element in productivity, namely the capital employed.*

CHAPTER TWO

The Source

If we were concerned about the future of our water supplies, we would not merely inspect the design and operation of all the faucets. We would look into conditions in the watershed area, and consider the adequacy of the reservoirs. Pension systems have something in common with this. But we must remember that the role of each pension plan is that of the faucet. In this section, we shall look to the source.

Whatever the type of plan, whether public or private, all pension and welfare payments must eventually come out of the gross national product.

Broad policies that have the effect of strengthening the economy are policies that in the long run will enable better pensions to be paid. Policies that merely commit the nation to vast pension outflows in the future, but contribute nothing to their source, will merely create conditions of economic stress, inflation and over-taxation.

It is here that we have to make a sharp distinction between the funded plans and the non-funded (or "pay-as-you-go" plans). These have totally different effects on the economy—the source.

The Old Age Security/Guaranteed Income Supplement (OAS/GIS) plan is the prime example of a non-funded plan. The CPP and QPP seem to be funded, but really they are not. Such reserves as they have accumulated are far below actuarial funding standards, and are destined soon to vanish if the present arrangements continue. The pension plans of many provinces for government employees, even though contributory, are non-funded. By contrast, the plans established by industry for its employees are designed to be fully funded, and their funding levels are carefully watched over by actuaries to see that they are sufficient to provide the promised benefits. The plans are further supervised by provincial watchdogs.

The pension plans of industry rely on their actuarial reserves to make good their promises to employees, while the public plans, by and large, rely on the future taxing power of the government. They have no reserves, or very little in the way of reserves, and everyone takes it for granted that the future taxing power of the government is a good asset. No one has really checked this out.

But the economy is not indifferent to the question of whether or not there are reserves. The reserves set up by the funded plans do many things besides providing pensions. They also provide the capital that the economy needs to generate production.

Production comes from a blending of three basic resources: land, labor and capital. In this study we shall not be discussing land, which includes raw materials, even though their indefinite availability cannot be taken for granted. We have already discussed the matter of labor, with respect to the size of the future work force in relation to the retirement-age population. We have seen that there are problems ahead, and that if all the pensions expected are to be provided, then the productivity of each worker will have to be increased. The most direct way to do this is through the provision of adequate capital.

To gain some impression of the role of capital in the community, perhaps it would be helpful to visualize the situation that would exist if the population of Canada were suddenly to double, without any other change. No increase in factories, houses or water supplies; no increase in electricity or schools; but twice the number of people. What a situation! Of course everyone's standard of living would go down—fast. Or we might look at it the other way. We might imagine that half of our existing productive capacity and social capital was suddenly removed by earthquake or enemy action. What a disaster! But if, instead of this happening suddenly, we were instead to let it happen gradually, would not the end result be the same?

So we have to be very careful about our sources of capital. Capital and productivity are inseparable.

Like the terms "gross national product" and "cost of living," and "total money supply," the term "capital formation" is often loosely used. Does the borrowing of money through bond issues to meet the current payroll or pay war pensions comprise capital formation? Or merely debt formation? Does the building of an aircraft carrier or a private residence (neither of which is used for the production of goods or services, though each of which has an economic function) comprise capital formation? Does the issue of bonds by a local authority to its own pension fund, thus relieving present taxpayers and enabling them to consume more now, so that future taxpayers will consume less later, comprise capital formation? But what if the money so raised is used to build a needed bridge or airport?

In the sense used in our analysis, the term capital formation implies the creating of both tangible and intangible assets including such items as research information, educational values, exploration and development costs as well as industrial plant and equipment, and social capital such as hospitals, water supply and transportation systems. It includes inventory and all such items as can be expected to have future or continued economic value, or to replace or maintain in useful condition items previously created.

Canada has an unusual need for investment capital. Consider these facts:

1. The surge of young people entering the work force over the near term is estimated to cause a *42.3% increase* in numbers working and seeking work over the 15-year period from 1970 to 1985.

The need for vast amounts of new capital to provide for a work force expanding in the short term is relatively greater in Canada than in such European countries as France, Germany and Britain where the figures corresponding to Canada's 42.3% range from 4% to 14%; or Japan (15%); or the United States (25%).

In the United States the capital investment required for each job ranges from $20,000 to $70,000, and averages $47,000 per job, according to former Treasury Secretary William E. Simon. The figure for Canada would be quite similar.

34

2. The radically different operating conditions and outlook of the energy industries as oil shortages loom ahead, energy prices rise, alternative sources have to be opened up, technology developed, pipelines built, and conservation measures pressed. Hydro power, nuclear power, solar power, coal liquifaction and gasification, oil recovery from tar sands, tidal and wind power are all voracious users of capital. More than 20% of all new investment needs to the year 1990 will be related to the provision of energy.

3. Urban redevelopment will need to proceed on a basis less wasteful of energy. Public transit systems, housing to meet the family formation needs of the tidal wave of young people, pollution control measures and other social and environmental needs will be very heavy users of new capital in the coming years.

4. Emerging world scarcities of raw materials require both stepped-up exploration for new sources and much research and re-equipment of industry to develop and use substitute materials.

The Economic Council of Canada, in its Twelfth Annual Review, had these very disturbing things to say about Canada's productivity and capital needs in the coming years:

"Canadian unit costs have risen substantially relative to U.S. costs since 1971 . . . The *rise in income* per employee of about 12% (in 1974) was accompanied by an actual *decline in real output* per person employed . . . Productivity in the total economy actually declined in 1974 . . . indeed, 1974 was the third consecutive year of deteriorating productivity performance." (Italic emphasis added.)

While pointing out that a part of the downward trend in productivity is associated with a shifting of economic activity towards the service industries, and that there will be strains on Canada's balance of payments, the Economic Council goes on to state:

". . . Substantial investments will be required in the late 1970's and early 1980's to improve Canada's productive capability . . . The growth of investment has not been particularly strong during the past decade . . . More sizable additions to the stock of capital will be necessary to sustain a given productivity growth rate . . . Important new investments are planned in . . . the development of energy resources and transportation . . . as well as restructuring industries threatened with international competition.

"What is required is an increase in overall investment and savings . . . The volume of domestic savings required . . . could be inadequate. Capital needs for the period 1975-85 will total $800-$860 billions (current dollars) . . . Corporations would presumably supply approximately 60% of the funds required . . . Reliance on foreign financing would likely be more substantial than in the past."

Returning to its theme about Canada's very unsatisfactory productivity performance and the deterioration of our competitive position, the Council states that in 1970-1974 unit costs increased by about 5% per annum in Canada, compared with less than 1% in the United States. "In the longer term view, this weakening of our competitive position is cause for deep concern," the Council concludes.

So we see that the need for more capital formation is vital to the whole economic health and strength of Canada. You cannot get good pensions out of an ailing economy for very long.

Dr. Arthur J. R. Smith, one of Canada's leading economists, had this to say in his June 15, 1976, address to the Canadian Electrical Association:

"We learned vividly and painfully in the 1930s that without good economic performance, there was simply no room or capability for improved health care or education or housing . . . Similarly, without good economic performance in the 1980s we will have little or no room in our system for . . . greatly enlarged social ambitions . . . also . . . ensuring adequate advances in the income of the elderly and the disadvantaged . . ."

Looking back to the good years of the first decade after World War II, Dr. Smith attributes our prosperity of that era to:

—Loosening the constraining networks of wartime controls.

—Fostering of both competition and new technology.

—Deliberate creation of conditions favoring new capital investment. "To make room for this greatly increased flow of resources to investment, we constrained government spending and slowed the rate of growth of consumer spending."

Since the mid-1960s, we have eroded or reversed all three of these policies, states Smith. "In the mid-1950s, the proportion of GNP going into new fixed capital formation was close to the highest in the world; by the mid-1970s, Canada stood 16th among the 24 OECD countries . . ."

". . . It no longer appears that productivity growth . . . represents a high priority in decision-making . . . In these circumstances . . . the Canadian economy is not functioning very well . . . We are experiencing slow growth, high unemployment and economic slack, high inflation, weak international trade and . . . troubling problems about . . . distribution . . . in a poorly functioning economy."

Smith adds this clincher: "The implications . . . are starkly clear: if we do not make room for . . . high savings and financial flows to new investment, there *is* no way to create new jobs at an adequate rate . . . We are caught in a bind because many sectors of the economy—as agriculture, forestry, fishing, mining, and energy—are becoming steeply more capital-intensive. Yet . . . we have not created a favorable environment for capital investment . . . Retained earnings have declined sharply . . . corporations are having to rely . . . on external financing just to maintain existing capital stock . . ."

Making a politically important clarification, he adds: "I would like to make crystal clear that . . . the importance of new capital needs . . . has nothing to do with . . . 'capitalist ideology.' It relates simply to the physical requirements of the means of production . . . equally relevant to all societies, irrespective of political structures and philosophies. Centrally controlled . . . economies such as Russia . . . or developing countries in Asia, Africa or Latin America, equally need large-scale new investment . . ."

South of the border, similar relationships between capital formation, productivity, unemployment, and welfare have been noticed. For example, Treasury Secretary William E. Simon had this to say in his May 7, 1975, testimony before the Senate Finance Committee:

"For many years our advantageous ratio of capital to labor has been acknowledged as the basis of the remarkable rise of the U.S. economy . . . Other nations during recent years have allocated a substantially larger share of resources to new capital formation.

"The reduced pace of capital investment in the U.S. economy has also been emphasized by Professor Paul W. McCracken, former Chairman of the Council of Economic Advisors. . . . He estimates that commitments in the United States during the 1970s are 22% below the level reported in the 1956 to 1965 decade.

"We are a consumption-oriented society, and this pattern has been developing for several decades. As a result, despite our high per-capita incomes, the accumulations of high gross savings flows required for capital investment are lower in the United States than elsewhere.

"Experience has demonstrated that inflation and unemployment problems have been created in part by capacity shortages. Many of our current difficulties are the direct result of the energy and raw materials strains that developed in early 1974 . . . The continuous deterioration of our international trade balance during the 1960s . . . was also at least partly the result of the loss of competitiveness of U.S. products . . .

"The private sector continues to be the best means of increasing capital investment in the United States . . . We must avoid legislation and regulation that is punitive of profits honestly earned. The result could only be that capital formation would be inhibited, and the real purchasing power of wage earners would rise more slowly. We must always be alert to the fact that profits translate into jobs, higher wages, and an increased standard of living for all of our people. We must also be concerned about the capacity of our capital markets to provide adequate financing."

Though Secretary Simon did not specifically point to the growing role of the actuarially funded private pension plans in providing this new capital, the connection is clear enough.

Equally plain should be the role of the expanding Social Security system in the United States, with its non-funded transfer-payment system of financing in America's transition from a "capital-oriented" to a "consumption-oriented" economy.

Martin Feldstein, professor of economics at Harvard University, has estimated that the establishment and expansion of the non-funded Social Security system has reduced by 30%-50% the incentive of private persons to save, and hence has cut deeply into the base of normal capital formation, seriously slowing the growth of the American economy in comparison with those of other leading industrial nations. Though this estimate may be a bit high, Feldstein's point is well taken.

What is Canada's position in this regard, and what does all of this have to do with pension funds and with the C/QPP in this country? To repeat:

1. The reserves accumulated under private pension funds are a major source of new capital formation, and are thus crucial to the economy as a whole.

2. The expansion of the C/QPP at the expense of private pension plans, or a shifting of emphasis toward the public plans, would thus tend to injure or debilitate the economy.

3. The assets in the C/QPP reserve fund are projected, on the basis of present contribution rates, to grow for a time but top out within only a few years, and thereafter to plunge down and disappear in an accelerating process of liquidation. This is the *reverse* of capital formation. To avert this, contribution (tax) rates will ultimately have to be raised, but even when the funding problems of the C/QPP have been faced, the result will still fall far short of the economically healthy effects of private funded pension plans.

Coming back to Canada's future capital needs, these figures were furnished recently by Dr. Douglas D. Peters, chief economist of the Toronto-Dominion Bank:

Needed in 1975 and used for:

Housing	$7.2 billion
Social capital	6.6 billion
Business capital investment:	
For energy sources	6.2 billion
For other industrial capital	17.1 billion
Total capital needed for 1975	$37.1 billion

In the decade 1976-1985:

Total capital needed for 1978	$52.1 billion
Total capital needed for 1982	$80.7 billion
Total capital needed for 1985	$116.5 billion

For the decade as a whole, a total need for $735 billion is foreseen, of which $155 billion would be for energy sources alone, $310 billion for other business purposes, $150 billion for housing and $120 billion for social capital.

In urging policies which will provide an environment favorable to a steady and continuous rate of economic growth, Dr. Peters stated in an October 1975 address:

"It is only with sustained growth that the projected levels of capital investment can be achieved without serious distortions in other sectors of the economy.

"The alternative is the much less desirable prospect of periods during which consumption would be severely restrained, enabling capital spending to catch up on those periods during which the total economy experienced little or no growth."

Looking five years further into the future, Dr. Arthur Smith in a June 1976 address anticipates that over the period to 1990:

—We will need to create "well over three million new jobs."

—Each new and existing employee will, on average, need to be equipped with a growing amount of fixed capital.

—Canadians will continue to demand an ever-widening diversity of choices.

On this basis, he projects these truly impressive figures:

| | Total Output | Total Investment | |
		Plant, Equipment	All Forms
		—$ billion—	
1975..........................	155	23	37
1976-80	1,000	170	260
1981-85	1,900	300	470
1986-90	3,000	500	770

Of the $6 *trillion* of total output projected for the 15-year period to 1990, about one sixth is needed for business plant and equipment; looking more broadly, one quarter is needed for all forms of capital investment.

To gather this capital together, Smith warns that we will need every kind of incentive to save and great prudence in managing our savings and investment, and even then will need "net capital inflows from abroad. If we fail, there will be many other nations poised to increase their development and welfare at our expense."

Where is this steady flow of investment capital to come from? In the year 1974, of a total of $35.8 billion:

—$15.2 billion came from capital consumption (depreciation) allowances.

—$10 billion came from retained earnings.

—$2 billion came from bank loans.

That leaves $8.6 billion to come from *domestic savings* and *foreign sources*. (Domestic savings include the growth of private pension funds, in addition to individual and other forms of savings.)

In 1975 and 1976, Canada, which already has a serious problem of excessive foreign ownership of its industrial capital, was still finding it necessary to import capital at the rate of $4 billion-$5 billion annually. To what extent can the growth of private pension funds help in this situation?

In pursuing this question, we requested Dr. John A. G. Grant, chief economist of Wood Gundy Ltd., to research the role of private pension funds in providing the capital needed by industry. Among the various findings resulting from this work, it emerged that:

1. Invested assets of private pension funds in Canada had grown by the end of 1974 to $25 billion, and can be estimated to have reached *$27.8 billion* by the end of 1975.

2. Annual contributions in 1974 to private pension plans amounted to $2.7 billion. (Of this, $2.1 billion went to trusteed funds and the balance to insured funds. Two thirds was contributed by employers and one third by employees).

3. In addition, $1.6 billion was contributed to the C/QPP.

4. As a proportion of the gross national payroll, contributions to the private pension funds had been advancing gradually until the establishment of the C/QPP, then dropped abruptly but again continued their gradual rise from a lower base. In 1974, a total of *5.73% of payroll* was flowing into all pension plans, of which 3.61% was going to the private plans and 2.12% to the C/QPP.

5. In addition to new contributions received, the private trusteed pension funds earned investment income in 1974 of $1.2 billion, paid out $800 million to current pensioners, and were able to make $2.2 billion available for new investments on behalf of current workers.

6. Adding the portion coming from the insured plans, the total investment capital available from the private pension funds in 1974 amounted to just under *$3 billion*.

What of the future? The amount of Canada's gross national product is inseparably tied to the total amount of capital employed by all of its industrial corporations.

Since new issues of bonds and stocks generally are the most

important area of new capital formation, it is of great significance to study the relationship between the future growth of pension funds and the amounts of capital needed to be raised through new bond and stock issues.

In making the projections that follow, Dr. Grant explored also the effects of both (a) a possible continuing encroachment of the public sector in expanding its share of the GNP, and (b) the possible continued growth, stabilization, or shrinkage of the flow of private pension fund contributions, depending on whether the C/QPP is dramatically expanded or not.

Taking a medium view of the outlook with respect to item (a), and postulating an economy in transition from rapid (current dollar) growth in the near term to a 4% rate of real growth with a 5% inflation rate after 1978, Grant projects a picture of economic growth for Canada which is illustrated in Chart XII.

If this degree of economic growth is to be achieved, then Grant's projection shows that the following amounts of new capital will have to be raised by new issues of stocks and bonds:

New capital to be raised:	1976-80	1981-85
	$ billion	
Through new bond issues	9.0	11.6
Through new stock issues............	11.3	14.5
Total..	20.3	26.1

At the same time, on a medium view, and assuming that there will be no radical change in the overall situation, private pension fund growth can be expected to furnish new capital for investment as follows:

New capital available from private pension fund growth:	1976-80	1981-85
	$ billion	
Bond purchases (non-government)......................	4.2	6.6
Stock purchases	8.9	14.1
	13.1	20.7

The vital role of the private pension funds in raising and channeling new capital into areas where it can best be used by industry stands out in sharp relief in these figures. *From 70%-80% of all the*

CHART XII

PROJECTED ECONOMIC GROWTH
(CURRENT DOLLARS)

$ BILLIONS

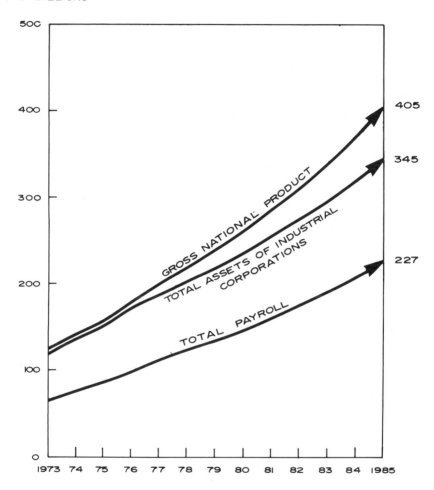

43

new capital needed by industry in Canada, and raised through new bond and stock issues, is expected to be furnished by the private pension funds.

It is of course not important whether these pension funds purchase new securities directly at the point of issue or whether, by buying already outstanding issues, they free up previously invested capital for placement in new issues. The effect is the same.

This heavy reliance of the Canadian economy on the growth of the private, actuarially funded pension plans as a source of needed new capital is a fact of life which has to be reckoned with in considering any proposals to change or expand the C/QPP in any manner which would result in a curtailment or slowdown in the growth of these private plans.

The basic importance of this stems not only from the amount of investment capital generated, but also from the difference between the funding and investment policies used particularly by the C/QPP and the private plans respectively. Each substitutes to a greater or lesser extent for the individual savings, the traditional source of capital, that existed before pension plans came into existence. But whereas the private plans develop reserves from their accumulated contributions, and channel these into the free capital markets so that the maximum economic return can be achieved, the C/QPP is at best only partially and temporarily funded, and is apparently on its way to becoming a straight transfer-payment (pay-as-you-go) system, making no contribution at all to capital formation.

Such reserves as have been accumulated in the past by the CPP have been confined to provincial bonds having only an ambiguous relationship, and in some cases no relationship at all, to real capital formation or any contribution to the GNP. While the QPP has done much better with its investments, its funding pattern is not basically different.

Nor is it desirable for the economy to be swamped and overwhelmed by the economic might of a single monolithic fund dwarfing all other institutional funds and concentrating too much power in one place, as would happen if these public plans were fully funded.

Chart XIII, opposite, shows the present outlook for the reserves under the CPP and QPP respectively. It is ghastly. After ris-

CHART XIII

FUNDS OF THE
CANADA PENSION PLAN
AND
QUEBEC PENSION PLAN
(CURRENT DOLLARS)

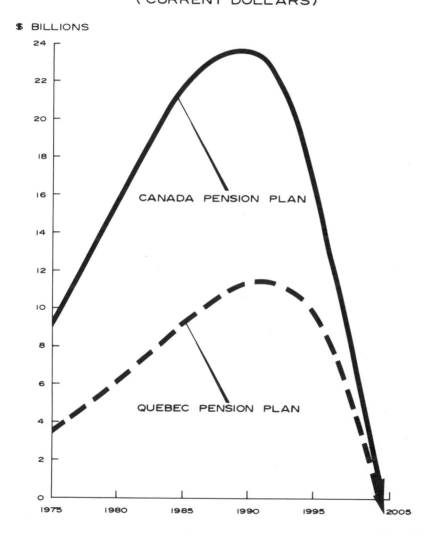

$ BILLIONS

CANADA PENSION PLAN

QUEBEC PENSION PLAN

45

ing for a few more years, if no changes are made, these temporary reserve funds will top out, then plunge in an accelerating frenzy of liquidation (*negative* capital formation).

This chart shows quite dramatically the funding dilemma faced by both the CPP and the QPP. They have deep problems. The basis of their financing does not seem to have been other than provisionally conceived from the outset. Though the choice of investments for the QPP funds has been well executed, the CPP story is in great contrast. With all funds channelled into provincial bonds, and their ultimate application not wholly visible, it is not possible to say that this partial and unusual pension funding operation has made or is capable of making a very impressive contribution to the strengthening of the economy or has assisted significantly in building the GNP. In no way can the C/QPP financing be regarded as a substitute for the private funded plans which its further expansion would displace.

It is against this background that we have to consider proposals to radically expand the CPP, having, as it would, the effect of sharply cutting back the benefits, contributions and growth of private pension funds and their ability to provide capital to the economy.

Dr. John Grant says: "Legislative initiatives which would sharply increase the benefits payable under the Canada and Quebec Pension Plans could, for instance, have an effect of this kind, which could wreak havoc in Canada's financial markets."

Dr. F. J. Brooks-Hill, an economist and investment analyst in Vancouver, has this to add: "In view of the rapid increase in the cost of maintaining the existing level of capacity, the cost of all resources and the cost of new construction, any curtailment in the flow of pension fund investments into the private capital market at this stage could have devastating economic effects."

In his study of the growth of pension funds in relation to Canada's capital needs, Grant concludes: "A decision by Canadians to substitute present for future consumption (which is the underlying implication of a switch from prefunding to pay-as-you-go deferred income plans) would either require a return to heavy reliance on foreign equity capital, with its undesirable implications for control of our resources, or would force a sharp slowdown in the rate of our economic growth . . . Even the power to pay the deferred incomes on a pay-as-you-go basis would be less."

From the viewpoint of its economic health and growth, Canada would thus seem to be better served by a continuation and strengthening of the present mix of diversified and actuarially funded private plans, improved in various ways as indicated later in this report, together with a C/QPP continued at its present scale but with its financing arrangements redesigned. We shall return to this subject later.

CHAPTER THREE

The Taxing Power
of the Government

Each year billions of dollars pour into pension funds, and flow out as pensions from government and private plans for the support of those entitled to receive them. The ostensible purpose of all of these money flows is to enable those whose age has advanced beyond the point of retirement, and their survivors, to continue to live in reasonable comfort.

When inflation erodes the dollar, the tendency is to react by increasing the pension so that its purchasing power will not be reduced. By this simple process of reasoning, the C/QPP, the OAP, the federal civil service, and various provincial and other (mainly governmental) pensions are adjusted without limit for changes in the consumer price index. With a 6% inflation rate and a retirement age of 60, this *doubles* the cost and value of the average pension. Even with a 4% inflation rate and a retirement age of 65, no less than 48% is added to pension values and long-term costs, given normal life expectancy.

When no funding (or only partial funding) is done, the full weight of these cost increases will not emerge for some time. The promise, the commitment, is made now, but only a small fraction of the cost is seen now. It is left for future taxpayers, for the next generation, to discover what has been done. But when pensions have to be funded, and costs incurred now have to be paid for now, there is more caution, more reluctance to become involved in these open-ended, unforeseeable costs.

This is why so many government plans are indexed without long-term cash-flow studies, with all caution as to future costs thrown to the winds, and why so few private plans are indexed. Under the federal Pension Benefits Standards Act, and the various provincial pension regulations, private plans must be actuarially funded, but the governments which impose these standards do not themselves meet the criteria they establish for the private sector from which their own economic strength derives. Instead of funding their pension obligations in a way that would build strength into the economy, they are regarded as "able to rely on their taxing power" to meet these commitments. On this, we shall comment later. And so a truly vast, unmeasured, unfunded liability is building up over Canada in the form of committed pensions, indexed without limit, while pension plan sponsors in the private sector tend to be rebuked for having failed to meet their social obligations to former employees by not following the example of their various governments in this regard.

For anyone interested in the possible dimensions of this phenomenon, it is instructive to look at the following three big-dimension examples recently provided by the United States, and then to relate these to the Canadian scene.

Example 1: The U.S. Social Security System

The 1973 report of the trustees disclosed that, as compared with the existing payroll tax of 9.9% (equally shared by employer and employee) for old age, survivors and disability benefits, there was a long-term actuarial deficit in the system of *2.98%* of payroll, so that payroll taxes would have to rise by *about 30%* over the long term to cover the cost of benefits committed.

One year later in the 1974 report, the 2.98% deficit had increased to *5.32%* of payroll, indicating that taxes would have to rise by *about one half* over the long term.

In the 1975 report, the 5.32% deficit had grown (on the "medium" projection basis) still further to *7.96%* of payroll, indicating that taxes will have to increase by *about 80%* over the long term.

As to the short term, the outflow for these indexed benefits is

49

now expected to exceed the income from taxes in each year, and the $44 billion trust fund to be totally exhausted by 1982—unless relief (heavier taxes) is provided soon.

The indexing of these benefits is technically faulty, but even the removal of the existing flaw in the basic benefit formula by new legislation will remove only about one half of the trouble. The other half still amounts to a deep and fundamental financial problem. The demographic bulge, discussed earlier with respect to Canada, is clearly mirrored in the long-term cost projections in the United States also. Starting small, the cost deficiency steadily widens from .88% of payroll in 1976 to 3.51% in 2000, then accelerates all the way to 16.69% in 2050 as the total payroll tax needed to support these non-funded indexed benefits rises to a devastating *28.59% of payroll!*

Example 2: The U.S. Civil Service Retirement System

Long regarded as an actuarially funded retirement system with its $28 billion fund invested in government bonds, and its benefits adjusted upward every time the CPI advanced by a cumulative 3% or more, the funding and costing of this plan proceeded on the basis of always looking *backward* at inflation, but never forward—always, that is, until its three-man board of actuaries in June 1975 felt compelled to show the facts to the world in their 52nd annual report, reflecting the status as at June 30, 1972.

Starting with the old style projection (ignoring future inflation), the Board of Actuaries reshaped the approach on the basis of future inflation rates of 3% and 4% respectively. The results of this more realistic view of the situation showed:

	With Inflation at:	
	3%	4%
A jump in net unfunded liabilities from $86 billion to.............................	$133 billion	$165 billion
A jump in annual employer costs from $6.8 billion to........................	$12.8 billion	$16.9 billion
Or, as a percent of payroll from 22.5% to	42.5%	56.0%

Even if the unfunded liability is left to grow indefinitely as the

50

payroll grows, so that the plan would no longer meet the minimum funding standards of the new Employee Retirement Income Security Act (ERISA) legislation as every private plan has to, the percent of payroll would jump from 22.5% to 33.9% or 40.0%, respectively.

There is no escaping the long-term costs of this plan merely by pretending that inflation does not exist or will not occur in the future. All that this does is to postpone, not avoid, the issue. In the introduction to its report, the board of actuaries states: "The provision for automatic changes in the benefits based on changes in the consumer price index has increased the liabilities of the system enormously in the last few years."

It declares in its closing paragraph: ". . . The costs to the government . . . are bound to rise sharply in the future. Obviously, if the current funding basis is to be continued, these future cost increases will have to be made up sometime . . . *the present approach to funding . . . will lead to spiralling costs in the future, not only in dollar amounts but a percentage of payroll.*" (Italic emphasis added.)

Note that these bone-jarring costs and cost increases are based on June 1972 payroll and CPI figures. What would they look like if recalculated today after four more years of record inflation?

Note also the enormous size of the total liabilities under this system, calculated in 1972 to be $281 billion (on the 4% inflation basis). This dwarfs and overwhelms the $28 billion of fund assets, wholly invested in bonds vulnerable to inflation. One has to search for such figures as the entire national debt of the United States to find a comparable figure.

Not also that this vast and rapidly growing liability relates *only* to the civil service plan of the federal government. It does not in any way overlap the also fast-growing $2.8 *trillion* liability under the Social Security System, or the vast, unmeasured, unfunded liabilities under state and local government plans, or for the armed forces.

Example 3: New York City

New York City's financial problem, which was in no small measure due to its indexed pension commitments, is not the only, but merely the most widely publicized example of tragic misman-agement of local government pension plans.

In a mood of helplessness before the weight of these unfunded and all-too-often unrecognized pension liabilities, the New York City budget director was exclaiming in 1971, "This pension cost is an enormous, invariable piece of granite which is insensitive to priorities and policy!" Four years later came the collapse.

New York City provides us all with a demonstration of the se-quence that occurs when capital funds raised through new bond issues are used to meet current expenses, when bureaucracy flour-ishes, and excessively costly pensions are committed but not prop-erly funded, all on the expectation that the taxing power of the government is an adequate resource.

A special commission has proposed to cut the benefits prom-ised under New York's pension plans so as to bring about a $3 bil-lion reduction in costs over the next 10 years, hoping that this will help to restore fiscal credibility to the city. With the union pension funds among the very few buyers of New York bonds, the fate of the city, and its employees are inextricably intertwined.

These three examples should be of great interest to Canadians since:

1. The OAS/GIS is wholly unfunded while the C/QPP bene-fits are only partially and temporarily funded, though all provide indexed benefits.

2. The old-style funding approach formerly applied with re-spect to the U.S. Civil Service Retirement System has much in common with the approach used in Ottawa in connection with the Canadian federal public service superannuation system.

3. The investment of much of the CPP cash flow into provin-cial bonds is being used to meet current expenses. Much of the New York City pension problem also applies in Canada.

The three situations just described are very large-scale and are indeed history-making in their impact. We are dealing here with the stuff from which the long-term economic history of nations is molded. In each of the examples cited, great reliance has been placed on the taxing power of a government as a basis of support for vast pension commitments to mature at a future time.

Immediately adjacent to Canada, the state of Washington is also in trouble with its pension costs. Appearing recently on television, Scott Blair, a Washington legislator, explained to the people of that state that its unfunded pension liabilities already exceeded $2.1 billion and were growing rapidly. Appealing for wide public support, he proposed heavy cuts in the pension plans for employees of the state, since any other course would require tax increases on a scale that he could not recommend. At one time Washington had established an actuarially funded system, but under difficult economic circumstances it omitted pension funding contributions when they became due, adopting instead the view that a government could always rely on its taxing power. The sequence of events after that took only a few years to develop.

This taxing power is being heavily and increasingly relied upon in Canada. In two of the cases mentioned it has already failed, with severe continuing social, political and economic effects, while in the other two cases the full implications of what has been committed are not yet widely realized, and the full burden on the taxpayer will not attain its ultimate gravity for some time. Furthermore, many aspects of the examples just described are presently being duplicated in Canada, or are proposed to be duplicated, with similar reliance on the taxing power of the government to extract an evergrowing price from future generations of taxpayers.

In light of this, we have examined the record of history to see whether the past can teach us something about the reliability of the future taxing power of a government, as a basis for providing benefits far into the future, and how far this taxing power can be pressed.

It may come as a shock to Canadians to think of nations being destroyed, empires collapsing, rulers being assassinated, wars being waged and lost, and the tide of history flowing into new channels as a direct result of overtaxation. In this country and in this era, one likes to think that nothing like that can happen here, that all of this, even though perhaps interesting, is irrelevant. But is it?

Glimpses of history: Overtaxation and collapse

The Fall of the Roman Empire

Edward Gibbon:

... During his [Caracalla's] reign, he crushed alike every part of the empire under the weight of his iron sceptre.

... Old as well as the new taxes were at the same time levied on the provinces. It was reserved for the virtue of Alexander to relieve them in a great measure from this intolerable grievance ... but the noxious weed, which had not been totally eradicated, again sprang up ... and in the succeeding age darkened the Roman world with its deadly shade. In the course of this history we shall be too often summoned to explain the land tax, the capitation, and the heavy contributions of corn, wine, oil, and meat which were extracted from the provinces for the court, the army, and the capital ...

... The tyrant's [Maximinus] avarice, stimulated by the insatiate desires of the soldiers, at length attacked the public property. Every city of the empire was possessed of an independent revenue, destined to purchase corn for the multitude and to supply the expenses of the games and entertainments. By a single act of authority, the whole mass of wealth was at once confiscated for the use of the Imperial treasury ... Throughout the Roman world a general cry of indignation was heard, imploring vengeance on the common enemy ... At length ... a peaceful and unarmed province was driven into rebellion ...

The system of Diocletian was accompanied with another very material disadvantage which cannot even at present be totally overlooked; a more expensive establishment and consequently an increase in taxes, and the oppression of the people ... The number of ministers, of magistrates, of officers, and of servants, who filled the different departments of state, was multiplied beyond the example of former times and ... when the proportion of those who received exceeded the proportion of those who contributed, the provinces were oppressed by the weight of the tributes. From this period to the extinction of the empire, it would be easy to deduce an uninterrupted series of clamors and complaints.

... An impartial historian, who is obliged to extract truth from

54

satire, as well as from panegyric, will be inclined to divide the blame among the princes whom they accuse, and to ascribe their exactions much less to their personal vices than to the uniform system of their administration.

Moses Hadas:

Under Maximinus, the demands of Rome upon its people and provinces grew more rapacious than ever. Herodian says that after reducing most of the notable houses to poverty, and finding the income obtained thereby small and insufficient for his purposes, Maximinus began to lay hands on the public treasuries.

Maximinus lasted as Emperor only four years, but his successors did little better . . . During those dark years, enemies breached the Empire's frontier on almost all sides . . . As the wars raged . . . the finances of the Empire utterly collapsed . . . Inflation gripped the money market, and the price of goods soared . . . Aurelian made matters worse by insisting that local officials must raise their town's customary tribute even when some of the town's lands were no longer revenue-producing . . . Diocletian increased the size of the army . . . broke up commands . . . This fragmentation called for an increase in officials and paper work; the result was a great expansion in the imperial bureaucracy. A note written in 288 . . . observes that "It is apparent that many persons . . . have devised titles for themselves such as administrators, secretaries, or superintendents, whereby they procure no advantage for the treasury but eat up the revenues."

. . . Diocletian's measures to make sense out of the Empire's monetary chaos were equally bureaucratic. As prices continued to soar unchecked, he issued an edict fixing maximum prices for goods and wages . . . the edict was incredibly detailed . . . But Diocletian's edict boomeranged . . .

. . . People were required to remain on their land . . . all men within the Empire labored and produced primarily for the benefit of the state.

C. Northcote Parkinson:

What had undermined the [Roman] Empire was the complexity of its own administrative machine. It was overtaxation which killed it in the West.

At the time of the Empire's collapse, the taxation of the provinces seems to have been crushing—too heavy in fact to be effective—and historians have agreed in regarding this as a principal cause of the disaster.

The French Revolution

George Lefebvre:
The immediate cause of the French Revolution was a financial crisis originating with the war in America . . . financed by borrowing . . . The deficit grew to such proportions that on August 20, 1786, Calonne sent Louis XVI a note declaring state reform imperative . . .

The treasury was now [in 1788] empty. Pensions had to be cut . . .

Agitation was especially pronounced in the countryside. There the tax burden was crushing; tithes and manorial dues drove the peasants to desperation . . . on all matters of taxation [the peasants were] solidly opposed . . . Tremors of the agrarian revolt could be felt well before July 14 . . . People were afraid . . . Officials let the villagers arm themselves for protection . . . [there was] fear of brigandage . . . panics broke out . . .

. . . . The Assembly enjoyed respect . . . on condition that it agreed with public opinion. Now everyone refused to pay former taxes and fees . . .

Now in arms, the people refused to pay indirect taxes and were slow in contributing to the others . . . municipal councils did not care to force them . . .

The treasury remained empty . . . Measures which even in normal circumstances had been used to obtain money while taxes were collected now failed . . .

Now there were new expenditures required by ecclesiastic pensions . . . In addition, besides its consolidated debt, the Old Regime had left huge arrears. The Assembly ordered payment of annuities (rentes) to begin again, and within two years 370 million livres were paid . . . floating debt rose one billion . . .

As early as October, 1789, the situation seemed desperate . . . The Bank of Discount, having in circulation 114 million livres in notes, of which 89 million were advanced to the state, declared itself out of funds . . . Under such circumstances paper money is the only resort . . .

Dupont de Nemours, Talleyrand, Lavoisier, and Condorcet predicted inflation and its ills. But political concern had joined financial necessity . . . A decline in the value of the assignat was inevitable . . . Before long the higher cost of living would produce effects not unlike those of hunger, stirring up [the] populace . . . French money depreciated in foreign exchange . . .

M. J. Sydenham:

Necker, the Controller-General, financed the war chiefly by loans, paying interest from further loans . . . and contrived to resign before credit collapsed . . . financial reforms had become imperative . . . [there was] public incredulity about the gravity of the situation . . . Existing taxation could not have been increased . . . The burden of direct taxation was already crippling those who paid it . . .

The Assembly of Notables . . . refused to accept any responsibility for authorizing new taxes . . .

The peasantry had another objective in attacking . . . [that was] the destruction of the manorial rolls which recorded the obligations to the seigneur . . . These included onerous payments such as the champart . . . equivalent to the tithe which alone accounted for about an eighth of the crop . . . They were a heavy burden upon men already bearing the weight of both royal and also clerical taxation . . . The manorial rolls were either destroyed separately or went up in flames with the house that contained them . . . The old order in the countryside could never be restored . . .

The payment of taxation was being refused, and life and property seemed everywhere in danger.

C. Northcote Parkinson:

[An] example of fatal taxation is to be found in the history of France . . . Taxes and tithes may have taken from 38 to 41% between them. At a certain point, probably short of 45%, the expenses of collection would have exceeded the value collected. Short of that again was the point of rebellion.

What the French government had done was to meet present needs by mortgaging its future revenue.

European imperial aims

C. Northcote Parkinson:

Coming to the history of modern times, we find that the first three to aim at ascendency on the imperial scale were Spain, the Netherlands, and France. As each failed in turn, excessive taxation played a part in its decline.

Some Far Eastern examples

C. Northcote Parkinson:

... An Indian scholar had pointed out that Eastern civilization ... was declining even in 1000 A.D. .... The immediate cause was, of course, excessive taxation. The Mogul emperors took a third of the gross produce, and worked on the theory that all land belonged to the crown; as a result vast tracts went out of cultivation.

If India's greater days were past, the same can be said of China. There the golden age of the Sung dynasty, the autumn period of Chinese culture, ended in 1279 ... The rule of the Mongols had a grandeur of its own, and they at least reunified the country. They taxed the peasants so heavily, however, that there was a resistance movement. After the revolution, the peasant leader became the first leader of the Ming dynasty.

George Lefebvre:

The Country [Japan] seemed prosperous in the seventeenth century ... But famines ravaged its people during the following century. Revenues ceased to flow to the state and to the daimyo. [Taxes including] duties, labor services, and land rents grew more oppressive to the peasants; currency weakened and dropped. The impoverished daimyo could no longer support the samurai who began to break away . . . Some adopted the errant life of the ronin, warriors who lived on the edges of society.

The British Empire

C. Northcote Parkinson:
    . . . The future historian will certainly look on the first decade of this century as the turning point . . . To maintain the impetus of British expansion would have involved providing two separate battle fleets . . . This price the British electorate refused to pay . . . a cause of the [British] defeat at Coronel . . .

[As World War I was approaching, the 1909 budget—controversial because it imposed heavy new taxes—provided 8,750,000 pounds for old age pensions, 3,000,000 pounds for the Navy, and smaller amounts for other purposes. This budget was ultimately defeated in the House of Lords.]

In his speech when presenting the budget of 1909, he [Lloyd George] said that his additional taxes were to wage implacable warfare against poverty and squalor. These taxes were highly significant, comprising a new super-tax and far heavier death duties. As the revolutionary HMS "Dreadnought" had been launched in 1906, starting an armament race in which Britain had only the smallest lead, some increase in taxation might have been thought inevitable. But it was not on the Navy that the money was to be spent. More of it was to go for old age pensions . . . The most significant thing about this legislation was—for our present purpose—its looking to the past. Spent on education or health, the money would have done something for the rising generation. Spent on armaments, it might have averted the First World War, or at least shortened its duration. Instead, its purpose was more sentimental—the care of the old. Only in a country with a slackened momentum could such emphasis have been possible.

In the long run, the incidence of rising taxes would have been enough in itself to bring the British Empire to a standstill . . .

Loss of influence follows from loss of strength . . . Britain was the country most heavily taxed in the years before World War I

. . . The two countries where taxation was the lowest were those whose influence increased the most.

Success in the modern age is to be measured by one's ability to extract the maximum subsidy from the State. To these ends, a new generation was to devote itself, leaving the British Empire to collapse more suddenly and more completely than any undefeated empire in the past; an example to the world of what excessive taxation can bring about and in how short a time.

What happens when direct taxation takes as much as 25% of the national income was first noticed by Lord Keynes in about 1923. It was he who pointed out that taxation, beyond a certain point, is a cause of inflation.

In his shrewd, erudite way, Dr. Parkinson traces the contrast between the influence in world affairs of a country with a strong economy and low taxes (as the United States was in 1938) and an overtaxed country which can do little to secure its wider interests or even to maintain peace.

"The first effect of a high peacetime tax rate is to reduce a country's influence in world affairs. The second is to be measured in loss of individual freedom," Parkinson states, quoting these words of Thomas Jefferson:

"To preserve our independence, we must not let our rulers load us with public debt . . . We must make our choice between economy and liberty, or profusion and servitude. If we run into such debts, we must be taxed in our meat and drink, in our necessities and comforts, in our labor and in our amusements . . . If we can prevent the government from wasting the labor of the people under the pretence of caring for them, they will be happy."

It should be noted that the American Revolution, a turning point in world history, was provoked by the extension of taxes to the colonies by England, and that it erupted first as a taxpayers' revolt.

Apart from questions of national survival, what we are concerned about in this book is the choice between profusion for one generation and servitude for the next, or economy for one generation and liberty for the next.

In interpreting the preceding highly condensed summary of what overtaxation has left in its wake in the past, and in weighing its relevance in today's conditions, we might do well to note these points:

1. The aggrieved peasants of earlier times comprised the great majority of the work force. In today's context, one might try substituting simply the word "workers."

2. In ancient times, when a potentially bad situation was developing, it was sometimes precipitated by a single bad harvest or drought. With an economy already taxed to the limit, there was no reserve strength or unused capacity to bear taxes. In the modern context, in the coming presence of huge, growing, unfunded, rigid pension rolls that have to be met year in and year out from current taxes on earnings, one can replace the words "bad harvest or drought" with "economic depression or unemployment"—which have the same effect in our present society.

3. While we tend to think of pension and welfare payments as something very modern, it is surprising how often in these examples we see the earlier counterparts of today's welfare system competing for their existence with the voracious demands of defense (or aggression), of bureaucracy, and of functionless, privileged idleness.

4. The ingredient that all of these have in common, the factor that seems to lead to the collapse of the system as a whole, is the fact that all *take out* from the gross national product, all *feed off* the economic base. No matter how necessary or desirable each may be in its own sphere, when the combined burden becomes too great for the economy that supports them all, then deterioration of the economic base itself sets in and collapse follows.

5. A strong, productive, fully employed, *understressed* economy is the best basis alike for defense, for the support of the old and the needy, and for influence in world affairs.

6. In the days of ancient Rome, it was the military who had the upper hand, and, together with the bureaucracy, eventually destroyed the very source of their own support through overtaxation. Today we read of the future overwhelming voting power, the coming political clout, of the rapidly swelling ranks of the retired population. Will these, then, be the future counterpart of the Roman legions, burdening down the productive sections of the popu-

lation to the point of collapse? Or will a modern counterpart of Diocletian's burgeoning bureaucracy do the same thing but more quickly? And what fateful tornado of taxation lies stored up in their deadly combination?

It is against this backdrop that one must consider the new luxurient crop of indexed, unfunded pension plans for public servants in Canada, and recall the pronouncement of Hon. Judy LaMarsh in introducing the Canada Pension Plan to the House of Commons on July 18, 1963: "In a public plan the contributor must rely upon the fact that *so long as his country exists* the continuous flow of contributions under such a plan will assure him of his benefit rights on his retirement." (Italic emphasis added.)

All the countries referred to previously still exist, but the leaders in those countries who placed unacceptable burdens on their taxpayers have long since been thrown off or destroyed or their glory gone. And who are Canadians but the children of those who freed themselves?

If there is one basic truth that stands out from all of these glimpses of history, and all that this author has seen in 47 years of heavy involvement in pensions, social security, manpower, defense, and the economics of welfare in Canada and other countries, it can perhaps best be stated in this way: The government protects pensioners best which best protects the *source* from which pensions are paid; and that source is the nation's economy. To plan in such a way as to weaken or overburden the economic base is to plan the collapse of the entire system.

There is a limit. The taxing power of the government is an asset that an actuary can use, and a pensioner rely on, only so long as the rate of tax is low enough to be acceptable. Even then, short-term contingency funds are needed. But when demographic and economic thunderclouds darken the horizon, and soaring taxes are threatened, it is time to think about other kinds of security.

CHAPTER FOUR

Pensions and Inflation

More than any other problem, inflation can truly be said to be the bane of the pension movement. Whether public or private, funded or non-funded, whether fixed in amount or based on career-average or final-average pay, whether indexed, variable, money-purchase, or otherwise designed, the adjustment of pensions (or the failure to adjust them) as a result of or in the presence of inflationary changes in dollar values, can have the most serious and even devastating effects both on individual lives, on pension costs, and on the economy.

How to cope with inflation is the subject of this section of this book, but to eliminate inflation is the only really satisfactory solution. Even at the price of severe, seemingly short-term sacrifice, the cooling down or rooting out of inflation must outrank almost every other social or economic objective and certainly every other pension objective. (We have already seen that excessive taxation is one of the causes of inflation.)

Just as it is possible to fail to correct for inflation, so is it possible to overcorrect for inflation. Each creates distortions and hardship. In this section of the report we shall examine what needs to be done within the pension field, what is being done now, and what remains to be done to cope with this ugly threat to the integrity of pensions.

History of inflation in Canada

Chart XIV, opposite, which shows the course of inflation in Canada since the year 1914, clearly mirrors the sharp upthrusts of two world wars and the sagging years of the depression and recovery between. Throughout all these traumatic years, when taken as a single span of time, inflation averaged 2% a year. Twenty years of fairly stable conditions followed, with inflation averaging 2½% a year. Only since 1970 has the pulse of inflation suddenly accelerated to a feverish 7% average.

Taking a succession of periods, all ending in 1976, this is the record:

Period	Commencing	Average Inflation Rate
62 years	1914	2.6%
26	1950	3.6%
16	1960	4.3%
6	1970	7.0%

The shorter the period up to the present time, the faster the average rate. There has been no peacetime period of inflation like that of the 1970s in Canada's history. This is the kind of inflation that can make a mockery of pensions. The very foundation on which savings, insurance, pensions, bond and mortgage investments and all similar long-term transactions are based is the concept of money as a store of value. When this concept is destroyed, and attempts are made to repair the damage on a piecemeal basis as has happened in Canada in recent years, widespread distortions result. Some few are advantaged, many are wiped out.

Inflation and the retirement age

When we turn the inflation graph inside out and present it as a history of the purchasing power of the dollar, we find that the dollar which would have purchased 100 cents worth in 1950 would have bought $2 worth in 1914, but only 79 cents worth in 1960, 60 cents worth in 1970, and only 40 cents worth in 1976. So a worker retiring on a fixed pension in 1950 would have suffered a 21%

CHART XIV

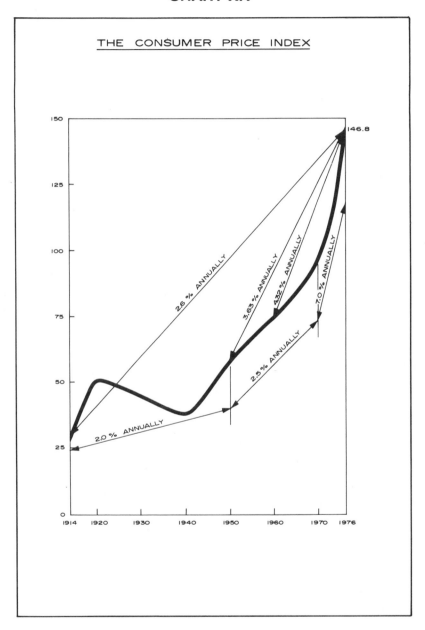

THE CONSUMER PRICE INDEX

shrinkage in the purchasing power of his pension in the first 10 years, a 40% shrinkage in the first 20 years and, if he still survived, a 60% shrinkage after 26 years of retirement.

The younger the age at retirement and hence the longer the expectation of life thereafter, the more severe is the impact of inflation. Too many pensioners have found out too late that they retired too early. Inflation has forced down their living standards or forced them back to work, perhaps after they have sold their homes and moved to a retirement location. Elsewhere in this book we shall be dealing with the trend to earlier retirement. It is sufficient here to note the adverse effects on the individual of early retirement in an inflationary environment.

Inflation as a funding problem

Employers faced with the problem of pension funding in a time of inflation are often trapped by its opposite effects on the assets and liabilities of the plan, forcing down bond and other asset values and driving up pay levels and pension liabilities. While theoretically better able to stand up to inflation trends in the long run, equity values have turned out in practice to be a very uncertain barrier of defense. (Adjusted for inflation, the Dow Jones Industrial average, at its depths in 1974, was barely above its 1906 levels.)

With nominal bond and mortgage yields at unprecedented levels to reflect the prospective loss of purchasing power of capital returned later, and with total investment portfolio yields rising to reflect these inflationary conditions, actuaries are faced with a dilemma in deciding how far to base cost calculations on an expectation that these present conditions will continue.

Until recently, federal tax regulations prohibited the use of an inflation allowance at all in cost calculations, a circumstance that impeded the sound funding of pension plans as required both by common sense and by provincial law. With this barrier now finally disposed of, there still remains a serious flaw in the regulatory picture which is causing financial strains to employers and distortions in benefit design and in the approach of actuaries to funding problems. This is the requirement that "experience deficiencies" (which are funding shortfalls arising from unusually

66

rapid pay increases, falling asset values or similar unexpected developments as recorded by the actuary in the course of his valuation) be funded over no more than five years.

Those who first drafted this requirement could never have contemplated inflation of the kind that has existed in the 1970s, or what this would do in throwing up experience deficiencies which, in the normal funding of a pension plan, are a measure of projected future experience as well as actual past experience. Had these effects been foreseen, it is unlikely that the lethal crunch of a five-year funding requirement, unprecedented and unnecessary as it is, would ever have been written into these provincial requirements.

The effects of this requirement are just about opposite to those which were probably intended. Instead of leading to the use of a strong actuarial funding basis (which would tend to reduce the emergence of experience deficiencies), and hence to a soundly operating private pension system, this requirement has instead driven many employers to choose benefit approaches which avoid exposure to inflation like the plague, and which are therefore less beneficial to employees. And it has driven actuaries to the use of funding methods other than those they would normally employ. In no other country does anything like this exist.

It does great harm. Canada's 15-year maximum rule for past service funding, which is severe enough though not unreasonable, would be quite adequate to deal with experience deficiencies along with other portions of pension costs not covered by future payments of the "normal annual cost" of the plan. The removal of the five-year funding requirement would simplify and restore flexibility to actuarial work and remove pressures from employers which presently militate against the adoption of pension plans. It works particularly against those types of plans that give the most protection to employees in a time of inflation.

Regulations, even of the most harmful kind, die very hard. If some niche must be preserved for the five-year funding requirement, perhaps the one rational place where it might survive could be in connection with a valuation based on the assumption of a plan shut-down. In this situation, there are no future benefit accruals to fund, and there may even be a scaling down of benefits already accrued where these are based on some future final-average pay. If, on the basis of such a test, assets are insufficient to cover benefit liabilities, a five-year funding of the difference might not be unreasonable. While not harming the choice of benefit design or funding method to any significant extent, this approach would eliminate any need for a pension benefit guarantee corporation along the lines adopted recently in the United States where nothing like the Canadian five-year or 15-year funding rules exist.

Here, then, is something that regulatory authorities can do to help the pension movement survive and digest the impact of inflation.

The income needs of old age

It has become orthodox in these times to think that all pensions should be adjusted at least in accordance with changes in the consumer price index, so that their purchasing power will be preserved in inflationary times. Many kinds of government pensions are so indexed, including those provided under the CPP, the OAS, the federal civil service and various provincial plans, though advance funding adequate for this purpose is rarely, if ever, provided. Though better funded, private pensions are almost never indexed, and there are some who are inclined to question whether private employers are not failing in their social obligations to former employees by not following the example of their various governments in this regard.

All of this is quite a reversal from the atmosphere that existed in 1954 when this author first introduced the idea of soundly designed cost-of-living pensions in the September-October issue of the Harvard Business Review, and designed the pioneer plan based on this principle for National Airlines, and later addressed the Canadian Pension Conference about this approach. In that era, and despite the safeguards designed into it, the whole idea met little but silent scepticism. It was an idea whose time had not come. Today, with all safeguards swept aside, vast commitments to indexed pensions are freely made with scant regard for their long-term effects on future taxpayers or on the economy. After all, why should pensioners suffer from an inflation? They have no defense. We owe it to them.

All of this takes it for granted that as age advances beyond the point of retirement, the need for cash income is fully sustained, and that the erosion of its purchasing power through inflation needs to be made good to fully the same extent as for a working family with young children and growing household needs.

The present consumer price index is not designed to reflect the living costs of those living in retirement. There has never been a separate cost-of-living index for retired lives; nor would it have shown everything that is needed, even if it had existed.

Since the purpose of pension systems is to provide income as age advances beyond the point of retirement, it does seem extraordinary that no recent statistical studies have been directed to an analysis of expenditure patterns with advancing age—not, that is, until for the purpose of this book, Statistics Canada kindly made a subdivision of the 1972 expenditure records of a sample of 532 families headed by persons aged 65 and over. These are the most recent available statistics. The results should be of intense interest to all who are concerned with the provision of income security to those in retirement. These are the highlights:

			Net Income		
Age Group	Number in Sample	Family Size (av.)	Per Family	Per Person	*1976 Equi- valent
			$	$	$
65-69	200	1.86	7,034	3,782	5,416
70-74	157	1.76	6,139	3,488	4,995
75-79	93	1.62	4,283	2,644	3,786
80 plus	82	1.58	4,016	2,542	3,640

*Net income per person converted to April 1976 by ratio of 1976 CPI to 1972 CPI and shown here for information only to give an impression of the relative income levels covered.

In testing to see how these average income figures related to what has been called the poverty line, as it existed in 1972, we have to bear in mind that there are many definitions of poverty. We must also remember that income needs vary from one location to another, that most statistics relating to poverty do not reflect exclusively the circumstances of the elderly, and that in dealing with this subject one can be more subjective or less so—one cannot be non-subjective. We must remind ourselves, too, that many of those who have retired own their homes and the physical assets they contain. (When this fact was taken into account, in a fairly recent study done in Melbourne, Australia, it reduced the percentage of income units below the poverty level, in that country, to 6% from 15%).

In some countries, the view is taken that if more than one third of the income is required to buy food, then poverty exists. In Canada, one measurement that has been adopted by Statistics Canada is based on the definition of "basic necessities," namely food, clothing, and shelter. If more than 70% of the income is spent on these basic necessities, then "low income" exists. A special Senate committee, looking into these matters in Canada in 1969, used a somewhat more generous definition of the poverty line, shown below. "The terms support level, low-income level, poverty level, and social-assistance level have been used extensively and at times interchangeably," states the Income Maintenance Directorate of Health and Welfare Canada.

After adjusting all figures to 1972 dollars, and interpolating between those for one-member and two-member families, the following comparison emerges between the incomes recorded by the 532-family-unit sample and the two minimum-income standards just referred to:

Age Group	Family Size	Recorded Income	Statistics Canada "Low Income"	Senate Committee "Poverty Line"
		$	$	$
64-69	1.86	7,034	3,319	4,033
70-74	1.76	6,139	3,179	3,864
75-79	1.62	4,283	2,982	3,628
80 plus	1.58	4,016	2,925	3,560

The basic characteristics of this sample thus reflect a shrinkage of income as age advances, but a continued margin of income, on average, above the poverty level at all ages.

With regard to the pattern of expenditures, it is instructive to note that the two largest items, shelter and food, both basic necessities, are the least affected by advancing age, as the table at the top of the opposite page shows.

With most other items, however, the picture is entirely differ-

70

Age	Expenditure for		Index			
			Per Unit		Per Person	
group	Shelter	Food	Shelter	Food	Shelter	Food
	$	$				
65-69	1,287	1,275	100	100	100	100
70-74	1,315	1,149	102	90	108	96
75-79	1,112	1,057	87	83	100	95
80 plus	1,168	950	91	75	107	88

ent. As age advances, clothing and footwear expenditures fall steadily to less than one half (though in the sample the purchase of furs advances with advancing age). Furniture costs fall to one third, floor coverings to one seventh, automobile-related costs to one sixth, while travel costs as a whole drop to less than one quarter. Taxes decline to one third, insurance and annuity premiums to one fifth, and union dues, fees and interest charges to one quarter.

Items that are more uniformly sustained than these include color television sets, vacation homes, permanent hair styles and shampoos, gifts and charitable donations, package holiday trips (but not above age 80) and reading materials. The fact that expenditure on these last-mentioned items is well sustained would seem to indicate that a comfortable standard of living is being maintained while overall cash income needs diminish. Even at the highest age, where cash income is lowest, net assets are still being added after all living costs have been met.

Medical costs, which might have been expected to increase sharply, in fact decrease somewhat, due no doubt to the various government medical plans.

The breakdown in broad classes of expenditure for items other than shelter and food is given in the table on page 72.

Even though the incomes recorded in this sample become significantly less as age advances, the ability to make gifts, add to assets, and purchase discretionary and luxury items, seems to be surprisingly well sustained. One does not see reflected here a picture of increasing hardship as age advances, but rather a natural outgrowing of some of the more expensive activities (such as those related to the automobile), a lessening of the need for new purchases of a long-term nature (such as insurance, annuities, furnishings—even clothing and footwear), a lifting of the tax burden,

	Age Group			
	65-69	70-74	75-79	80 Plus
	$	$	$	$
Expenditure item (annually)				
Taxes (personal)...........................	908	796	311	301
Security (insurance, annuities)........	230	82	68	46
Dues, fees, interest, lawyers	158	73	104	39
Household operation.......................	291	252	202	188
Furnishings, equipment	264	197	132	97
Clothing, footwear...........................	425	311	212	184
Personal care (hair care, toilet needs)..................................	154	111	91	87
Smoking, alcoholic beverages........	247	194	134	132
Medical, health care........................	220	173	149	164
Travel, transportation......................	615	370	336	137
Recreation, reading, education	266	211	156	142
Gifts, charitable contributions	281	278	182	183
Increase (decrease) in assets for year...............................	**368**	**714**	**(67)**	**255**

The discretionary expenditures mentioned above, which are included in these figures, are as follows:

	65-69	70-74	75-79	80 Plus
Color television sets	28	33	31	33
Furs...	16	13	16	20
Vacation homes................................	14	6	6	16
Permanents, shampoos	55	40	33	33
Package holiday trips.......................	53	35	31	7
Christmas, birthday gifts, donations	195	167	128	145
Reading materials............................	44	42	33	38
	405	336	278	262

and, on the other hand, a greater emphasis on such pursuits as reading, television and family pursuits where the costs are much less. This is a time for the gradual consumption and enjoyment of items already acquired.

What does all of this tell us about the need for indexing pensions?

1. The need for basic necessities such as food and shelter con-

tinues without significant reduction throughout life. These two items together accounted for less than 40% of the age 65-69 total expenditures of those covered in the sample, but close to 50% of their total "current consumption" expenditures.

These percentages increase, however, as income reduces, regardless of age, and conversely they are reduced as income increases. In dollar terms, these items represent a hard core of living costs which do not change very much with changes in age or income, but which do change with inflation.

That portion of the retirement income which relates to these *should be sustained* at its full purchasing power as a high priority item in any comprehensive pension system or combination of systems.

2. As to the remaining items of expenditure, the information provided by this sample indicates that as age advances, and the natural level of activity is reduced consistently with maintaining a good standard of living, there is less need for cash income.

This is not to say that, as age advances, the overall needs of the elderly become less. Their psychological and communal needs increase. Loneliness, vulnerability to accidents, special housing and creative use of time become pressing problems which are referred to elsewhere in this report. Here we are concerned merely with the cash income, and it is in this area that the evidence provided by the present sample indicates a diminishing need as age advances.

Notwithstanding much current thinking and government policies, the full and unlimited indexing of pensions above the basic first 40% of income required for necessities could be a mistaken practice and an unnecessary and expensive luxury.

It is of course possible that further research in this field, based on more extensive data, would change these conclusions. They do, however, stand up to the test of common sense.

Considering the vast future amount of money in the form of taxes to be extracted from workers and benefits to be provided to the elderly, amounting in all to a large slice of the entire gross national product, does it not seem to have been an oversight that a commitment to index pensions without limit could have been made without any research into the needs of the retired? In this, Canada is not alone.

Is it not also evident that, both in adding consumer income where the need is less, and in raising taxes to pay for the cost of this and hence increasing labor pressure for compensatory pay increases, these steps being taken so hastily to offset inflation are likely to increase it?

Apart from the lack of demonstrated need for the full and unlimited indexing of pensions, there are certain general arguments founded in social justice that weigh heavily against it.

In the 1950s, when the idea of indexing pensions was first developed, inflation was not the rampaging menace that it has since become. From the beginning of the history of the consumer price index there have been only brief periods of severe inflation. In the United States, over the period since the beginning of the present century, a 2¼% compound growth curve could be fitted reasonably well to the CPI, and in the period from 1950 to 1965 its growth rate averaged only 1.9% annually. Canada's experience was very similar.

In this period there was no oil shortage or quadrupling of prices imposed from abroad, and very little concern about raw material shortages, pollution, or other environmental problems. Rachel Carson had not published *Silent Spring*, there was no Club of Rome and no concern about the limits to growth or population pressures. America had the problem of storing its bursting grain reserves, and land was being taken out of production with government assistance. Mankind did not seem to be at any particular turning point.

Looking back, these seemed to be halcyon days of innocence and naivete when the extrapolation of long-observed trends could be done with a reasonable feeling of confidence. In promoting the idea of cost-of-living pensions, we could at that time see no reason to think that these might one day place their recipients, along with others receiving indexed incomes, in an unfairly advantageous position. Today it seems that this is indeed the prospect, and we have to rethink the whole idea of indexing pensions and other incomes.

To the extent that an inflation is imposed on a nation from abroad (as has recently been done by the oil-producing nations), is it fair to exempt one segment of the people, so that these can carry on as though nothing at all had happened, while the remainder must bear two burdens? Must they bear the direct burden resulting from the externally imposed inflation and *also* the added tax or similar costs of providing the higher pensions and incomes of the protected segment? Similarly, to the extent that inflation is caused by higher costs arising from the drying up of resources, the battle against pollution or other environmental factors, or the defense of the nation, this reflects a burden that should in fairness be shared by all.

In a period of unlimited resources, rapidly increasing productivity and steady increases in "real" standards of living, this problem of distortion through indexing was not significant. But population pressures are mounting throughout the world, pointing to an era of higher food prices and higher costs of substitute forms of energy have to be faced with all their repercussions throughout the economy. These fundamental changes bring consequences that should be faced and borne by all. To exempt a privileged section from their effects is to create a transfer of wealth to them which was not intended.

What then should be the future of indexing? It seems that we must begin to consider a form of adjusting pensions and other incomes that recognizes something less than the full extent of the changes in the CPI, or the indexing of something less than the full pension or combination of retirement income, so that the objectives of these adjustments can be accomplished in a manner that is fair to all.

The indexing of public and private pensions

The approach to indexing public and private pensions in Canada varies widely. OAS, the C/QPP, the federal civil service plan and some of the provincial plans are fully indexed without any limit. A 6% and an 8% limit exists in certain provinces. Vestiges of a 2% limit remain in some governmental and semi-governmental plans. Some provincial and many private plans are not indexed at all but are subject to various kinds of ex gratia ad hoc catch-up adjustments.

It is notable that where public plans have been indexed without limit, no corresponding attempt has been made to fund in advance for the extra costs that this implies, or indeed to measure or project the extent of the resulting extra tax burden. No private plan operating under the guidance of the Canada Pension Benefits Standards Act and its provincial counterparts could behave in this way. Only a governmental plan, relying perhaps too blindly on its future taxing power, and not subject to the discipline of the funding standards legislation, could risk this kind of step, committing a future generation of taxpayers without its knowledge to the cost of pensions destined to increase unnecessarily, and as it now appears, unfairly.

What are these extra costs? If a male were to purchase an annuity at age 60 with the monthly amount increasing each year from that time on until the end of his normal life expectancy, the *extra* cost due to this periodic increment would be:

> 36%, if the annual increment is 3%
> 52%, if the annual increment is 4%
> 73%, if the annual increment is 5%
> 98%, if the annual increment is 6%
> More than 100%, if the annual increment is more than 6%.

So the federal government, for example, in deciding to index the pensions of its employees without limit, may very easily be *doubling* the value (and cost) of these pensions. For the first layer of pension, the employee pays 6½% of his salary, and the government pays a somewhat similar amount. For the second layer, as the machine is now set up, each side pays a maximum only 1% of salary, with the entire (unknown) balance to be borne by the general taxpayer!

Nor is that all. At earlier retirement ages the extra cost is still higher. If the retirement age is 55, as is provided for under the federal civil service plan for those with sufficient qualifying service, the *extra* cost becomes:

> 39%, if the annual increment is 3%
> 58%, if the annual increment is 4%
> 82%, if the annual increment is 5%
> 111%, if the annual increment is 6%

If it can be said that the value of the plan was doubled by this step, it is not just the 6½% that was doubled, but the whole 13% of payroll. So by paying in an extra 1% of his pay, the civil servant collects what is probably the equivalent of a 12% pay increase. The exact value of this "pay increase" is, however, unknown and unseen either by the civil servant or by the future taxpayer whose money is thus committed, and for which no fund exists. In this transaction, the civil servant receives something else too, and that is complete economic protection from the unknown. How about the taxpayer? A *double* impact from the unknown? Did anyone look into this? It is of particular interest that this change was rushed through at a time when inflation was nearing 10% per annum.

In looking over the series of *extra* costs shown above, it is interesting to note that each 2% increase in the assumed inflation rate *doubles* these extra costs. Can you imagine what a double-digit rate of inflation, if it were to continue, would do to all of these very large but hitherto unseen shifts in value?

An approach to adjusting pensions after retirement

One of the fascinating things about the employee benefit field is that, although it is really quite simple and straightforward in its essentials, it can be made to seem so complicated, so technical, so esoteric and so abstruse, that only actuaries could hope to understand it. And even the actuaries must be constantly on guard against being leg-roped in beta coefficients, incompatible computer language and $q_x^{(w)}$ factors, drowned in an ocean of numerals and writhing symbols, or fogbound in the amendments to a maze of indecipherable legal documents unpunctuated except with circular cross-references. Small wonder that broad perspectives in this field are difficult to come by!

In their tireless creativeness, actuaries have tried to bring relief to pensioners suffering from inflation while at the same time avoiding cost commitments that can roast the next generation of taxpayers, or the present generation of stockholders, or the financial vice-president, or put the company (or the country) out of business.

Their ingenuity thus challenged, actuaries have come up with these solutions, among others:

—To index pensions with a cap of 2% or 3% annually, this

limit to apply (a) each year separately, or (b) cumulatively.

—To index pensions with a delayed action, so that the pensioner takes the knock either for the first x years, or for the first y percent, and then the plan takes over the further inflation risk (like auto insurance with a deductible).

—To commit the plan to index pensions for no more than three (or five) years ahead; after that it's a new ball game.

—To index only one half (or other fraction) of the pension, or to adjust the whole pension by only one half of the movement in the index.

—To index only the first so many dollars of the starting pension, the remainder to be level.

—To index the pension upward until a stated limit of income is reached, but no further; alternatively up to a stated limit of cost.

—To fix the annual increment from year to year, regardless of inflation, as either (a) a set percentage compounding annually, or (b) a set dollar step each year (like simple interest), thus making the cost of the pension mathematically determinable.

—To hitch the amount of monthly pension to the asset values of the pension fund, so that the pensioner can participate in (enjoy?) the up-and-down action of the stock market along with the up-and-down action of his grocery bill (once thought promising, but not lately).

—To spring any of these systems off a final-average-earnings based pension or an updated career-average or other pension.

—If a final-average benefit formula is not used, to index each unit of the career-average or flat benefit from the year when it was accrued to the time of retirement, as well as after that time.

—To use an indexed pension based on a cut-down formula as a *minimum* benefit in a plan otherwise providing a generous fixed-dollar pension.

—To provide the retiring employee the *option* of an indexed pension on a cut-down formula, or a fixed pension on a more generous fixed-dollar basis.

—To use some other combination of two or more benefits, including some element selected from the above methods.

—To use a wage index in place of the consumer price index in applying any of the above methods.

—To make only ad hoc adjustments, as decided from time to

time by the employer or in bargaining with the union (the forms of these adjustments occupy another list as long as this one).

With ingredients such as these to work with, the permutations and combinations of ways to adjust pensions for inflation are almost endless. While most are capable, with proper design of detail, of providing relief where it is required, none need go as blindly overboard as full, open-ended, unlimited, unmeasured CPI indexing. Only a government can afford to throw future taxpayers overboard with that kind of careless abandon.

Consider for example the contrasting *extra* costs which arise from the following choices, all of which are based on retirement at age 65, and all of which assume that there will be a 6% annual increase in the pension. The first column of the tables below takes these increments forward on a simple interest basis and the second column on a compound interest basis. Both columns show the effects of a three-year or a five-year delay in commencing these increases.

Extra cost, as percentage of basic pension cost, when increments commence with:

	Simple	Compound	Difference
No delay	46%	86%	40%
3-year delay	30%	57%	27%
5-year delay	22%	42%	20%

With retirement at age 55, the extra costs are higher, and the cost difference widens even further:

	Simple	Compound	Difference
No delay	60%	111%	51%
3-year delay	42%	79%	37%
5-year delay	34%	62%	28%

Instead of a *doubling* of the pension cost through indexing, as occurs with the first line of figures, the extra cost can be cut to a more manageable fraction by providing for a delay, or a "simple interest" form of increase, or both. If the rate of pension increase is limited to 3% each year, all of the figures become smaller and less widely separated, as the table at the top of the following page demonstrates.

**Extra cost as % of basic
pension cost, when increments
commence with:**

	3% Annual Limit		
	Simple	**Compound**	**Difference**
		(Retirement Age 65)	
No delay	23%	33%	10%
3-year delay	15%	22%	7%
5-year delay	11%	17%	6%
		(Retirement Age 55)	
No delay	30%	40%	10%
3-year delay	21%	29%	8%
5-year delay	17%	23%	6%

What is the merit of a delay, or a "simple interest" form of annual increment? First, these methods split the cost and risk of inflation between employer and employee on the basis of letting the individual carry the first part of the risk, then underwriting the excess as is so widely done in the automobile- and medical-insurance fields. Secondly, by choosing the less costly "simple interest" form of increment, relatively less emphasis is given to pension increases as age advances and monetary needs decrease.

Finally, these devices bring the cost of post-retirement adjustments within reach of private plans, and enable adjustments to be made where none is being made now.

There are of course other fruitful ways of approaching this problem. Remembering what we have just learned about expenditures as age advances, we must also consider:

1. The need for an indexed "bottom layer" of income to cover the basic needs for food and shelter.

2. The presence of both the OAS and C/QPP which are fully indexed. Perhaps these already provide that "bottom layer." Providing well above 40% of net income from full-time work, they generally cover more than just the two basic needs with fully indexed income.

3. The indicated decline in cash needs with advancing age for items *other than* food and shelter, hence the lesser need for post-retirement adjustments in areas above the OAS and C/QPP levels. Whether there is *any* need depends on the rate of inflation.

From the expenditure sample described earlier, we might derive something along these lines:

Overall average cash needs shrink 2% a year as age advances. However, 40% of needed income (for basics) does not shrink at all. Therefore, the balance shrinks 3.3% a year. Hence:

—The basic 40% must be fully indexed. (This is already more than taken care of by OAS and C/QPP.)

—The balance needs to be protected only with respect to any inflation *in excess of 3.3% a year.*

Therefore the job for private plans is to offset any excess of inflation above 3.3% annually.

This is a new approach, not listed among the methods enumerated earlier. While the rough outlines of its logic seem clear enough, and its cost may turn out to be reasonable, the fact that there is no limit on the extent of the inflation risk (in excess of 3.3%) would certainly cause hesitation among employers. So in practice some limitation would be needed. Instead of asking the employee to carry the *whole* inflation risk for the first few years, and then shifting the whole risk after that (possibly with safeguards) to the employer, this approach asks the employee to carry only the bottom layer of the inflation risk on income *other than* the basic OAS and C/QPP income (which is fully protected). The private pension would thus bear the brunt of the "excess" inflation risk (up to acceptable limits) on income above that. In this way, the needs of the retired employee would be met and the purposes of the plan would be achieved.

If inflation can be slowed to a rate of 3% or less, there would be no extra employer cost, no adjustments in the private pension, and those living in retirement would be well provided for. While diametrically opposite in principle to indexing up to a 2% or 3% ceiling, as was done in the first generation of indexed plans, this approach puts the extra money where it is needed, not where it is not needed. It corrects the weakness that caused the earlier generation of plans to give way under the pressure of double-digit inflation. What is logical, and what happens in real life, however, are often quite different. If there is a defect in the approach just outlined, it could lie in the unpredictability of the extra cost. Though substantially less, under all circumstances, than the cost of unlimited indexing, it could certainly fluctuate. The table overleaf shows the extra cost for post-retirement adjustments expressed as a percentage of the basic pension cost.

Retirement	Sustained 6% Inflation		Sustained 3% Inflation	
Age	Full Indexing	Approach Outlined	Full Indexing	Approach Outlined
65	86%	48%	33%	None
60	98%	57%	36%	None
55	111%	66%	39%	None

While the present illogical requirement for funding experience deficiencies over five years, criticized earlier, continues to exist, an employer subject to its terms would be hesitant to write this provision into a formal pension plan for fear of being painfully trapped between a capricious regulation and an inflationary fluctuation. Instead such a provision would probably tend to be encased in limits or used as a guide for ad hoc adjustments, not committed in advance. But if pensions are to do their job, this is the kind of adjustment that is needed.

What, then, of the position in which the federal public service superannuation system finds itself, with its early retirement and unlimited indexing provisions? A bit like a schoolboy caught with his hand in the cookie jar? Somewhat, but not exactly. It was approved, after all, by Parliament in the normal course of its business and supported by spokesmen of all parties. But governments can make very, very bad mistakes in the pension field, and when this happens there is nothing to do but to correct the error.

It is only a few years since Congress in the United States inadvertently injected a defective indexing provision into that country's Social Security system that had the unintended effect of causing new pensions to grow at a rate much faster than was called for by the rise in the consumer price index. It took some time to recognize the error, and identify the exact cause of the trouble. While this was being done, and a new formula designed and tested, the financial problems of the system grew steadily worse, so that in 1976 it was officially estimated that it would take about an 80% increase in the present 9.9% tax rate to get the system back into a sound long-term financial balance. Of this cavernous deficiency, fully one half, or perhaps two thousand billion dollars, comes from the flaw in the indexing formula that was unrecognized when it was enacted, and wholly unintended. There was nothing to do but correct the error, and in 1976 draft legislation was sent to Congress to do this. One has to recognize the political courage of a President having to take this step in the face of an impending election. But some things are simply too big not to be corrected. This full, unlimited indexing of pensions is in that class.

So, in Canada also, we are faced with the situation of a federal government having enacted legislation providing pensions to civil servants which are:

—Fully indexed without limit, and without delay.

—Out of step with the normal practices in the society within which they exist.

—Additional to the OAS and C/QPP benefits (the indexing of which on their present scale can be more easily defended); hence—

—Unnecessary, in the form enacted.

—Unable to be justified on general principles.

—Unmeasured as to cost, but with a very large cost potential, perhaps $500 million annually or more at this time, and growing as an *extra* long-term cost to taxpayers.

—Totally unfunded, hence casting a heavy shadow on taxpayers of all future generations.

—Dangerous in their precedent-setting role, and already copied in certain provinces, similarly without adequate study of cost, necessity, or other implications.

Here, as in the United States, it would seem evident that a very large mistake has been made—understandably enough, but nevertheless a mistake that needs correction.

CHAPTER FIVE

The Public Pension Plans

". . . It is possible to see the outlines of a new purpose: one based on self-conscious maturity . . . that seeks to redefine the self and the liberal society on the only basis on which they can survive . . . [that is] on a recognition of the limits of our power, individual and social, to deal with unlimited appetites and wants.

". . . Within limits, men can remake themselves and society. But the knowledge of power must coexist with the knowledge of its limits. This is, after all, the oldest and most enduring truth about the human condition."

Daniel Bell,
professor of sociology,
Harvard University

One of the remarkable things about the public pension systems in Canada is that no one has ever measured the extent of the commitments that exist now under them—commitments that will have to be made good by future taxpayers—or where these commitments are going. Canadians are not periodically jolted to read in the newspaper that the combined unfunded liabilities that exist today under the OAS/GIS and the C/QPP have now swollen to

$400 billion, whereas the total assets held amount to no more than $12 billion-$13 billion.

Not at all. Here, in the True North strong and free, our perspective is different. In Quebec, the Caisse de depot et placement du Quebec presents its proud report showing an exemplary diversification of its $4 billion, producing an 8.11% yield, and feels that "it can look forward confidently to the management of increasingly larger funds in the future." A dazzling performance!

Across the rest of Canada, like a beautiful lady sawn into 10 sections to satisfy each of her 10 suitors, but with one section removed, the Canada Pension Plan can boast of no coherent investment policy at all. Tax revenues not used currently to pay out benefits are simply placed at substandard interest rates in nonmarketable, callable, 20-year provincial bonds.

No one seems to know quite what happens to all of the money after that, except that a large part of it is used for "the general purposes of the province." True, there is a brief list of items of social capital and the odd economic asset or two that were built in a few provinces, mainly in the earlier part of the 10-year period of this peculiar pension funding exercise, but that is about all, and one cannot escape the impression that this is a $9-billion-reserve fund that has not only lost its way, but lost its identity as well.

"The CPP has become the backbone of provincial debt financing," states its advisory committee, pointing out that in the four years to March 31, 1974, the CPP had furnished 38% of all provincial borrowing. "A bloody rip-off!" is how a highly informed non-government observer in Ottawa described this procedure. Whichever way it is viewed, it does not stand up to the normal tests of a pension funding operation.

". . . The savings which other Canadian provinces make with respect to public service debt because of the preferred rates they obtain on borrowings from the CPP are realized effectively at the expense of the overall return on pension plan assets." So states the presumably impartial report of the more successful Caisse de depot et placement du Quebec. This means, of course, that the tasks of the respective provincial treasurers and the present burdens of provincial taxpayers are being made temporarily lighter at the expense of those who will have to pay the increased taxes which will be needed in due course to keep the soon-ailing CPP going.

For the party will be over soon. It is only in these first few start-up years that the 3.6% CPP tax rate is more than sufficient to pay current benefits. As each year passes, the pension rolls are building and the average amount of each pension is increasing. By June 1975, almost 700,000 Canadians were drawing benefits from the CPP alone, and the number was increasing by more than 100,000 each year.

The outflow of benefit dollars was growing proportionately even faster:

Fiscal Year Ending	Benefit Outflow $ million
1971	89
1972	144
1973	206
1974	279
1975	400
1978 (estimated)	1,400
1980 (estimated)	2,000
1990 (estimated)	6,750

Within a very few years this rising tide of benefit outflows will have overtaken the inflow of revenue from the 3.6% tax, and then the moment of truth will arrive.

It is one of the interesting aspects of the present CPP financing arrangements that the provinces, having borrowed the temporary excess of CPP revenue over expenses, thereupon borrow the interest they would normally pay on the first borrowings, so that the debt simply compounds and nothing is paid back: a provincial treasurer's delight!

So stimulating to the imagination is this method of investing a pension fund that the chief actuary in the Department of Insurance in Ottawa, in preparing his actuarial reports on the CPP, has regularly included it when projecting the future outlook of the CPP finances. Of the three alternative funding methods projected, this is one. Perhaps with tongue in cheek, he has dignified these three methods with the names Fund A, Fund B and Fund C.

The strangest things can happen when one is making actuarial cost projections and doing policy research work. Sometimes a dar-

86

ing idea, dreamed up merely to set an outside limit, or to test a crossover point, or to show how impractical a particular course of action would be, is seized upon and taken seriously by policy makers, and long and earnest discussions are based on it, and a whole world of politics springs up around it, while the research man wishes he had never let it be seen outside his own office.

Such, one suspects, may be the situation with Funds A, B and C. After all, these are nothing more than three of an infinite number of ways of paying for the costs of the Canada Pension Plan. But there they are, sitting up nice and pretty in the official actuarial reports, like three seductive girls in a beauty contest, inviting inspection and selection.

One of the major decisions of the decade in Canadian finance will soon have to be made, either in choosing one of these or in dreaming up something different. This selection will have the most far-reaching impact on:
—Federal-provincial relations;
—Provincial tax rates;
—Provincial spending and borrowing arrangements;
—Present and future CPP tax rates;
—Individual equity and windfalls from the CPP;
—Intergenerational subsidies between people;
—The capital markets; and
—Private enterprise.

It would therefore be a good thing if Canadians were to become somewhat familiar with the options that lie open, and to get some sense of what is quietly buried in the equally inviting looking, though statistically dry presentations of Funds A, B and C (as in the table on page 88).

So to help us get a sense of the meaning of these figures, let us take a comfortable but imaginary journey together into the future, riding through the decades with each of these projections in turn, so that we can see what the scenery might look like.

Hold on tight.

Summary of fund projections for the existing Canada Pension Plan

| | | Fund A | | | Fund B | | | | Fund C | | | |
| | | 3.6% Contribution Rate | | | Cash Flow to Provinces Decreases until Zero | | | | Cash Flow to Provinces Decreases until Negative and Equal to Interest on Fund | | | |
Calendar Year	Benefits and Expenses Millions $	Contributions Millions $	Cash Flow to Provinces Millions $	Fund Billions $	Contribution Rate %	Contributions Millions $	Cash Flow to Provinces Millions $	Fund Billions $	Contribution Rate %	Contributions Millions $	Cash Flow to Provinces Millions $	Fund Billions $
1975	629	1,290	660	9.2	3.60	1,290	660	9.2	3.60	1,290	660	9.2
1976	855	1,451	596	10.5	3.60	1,451	596	10.5	3.60	1,451	596	10.5
1977	1,110	1,632	522	11.8	3.60	1,632	522	11.8	3.60	1,632	522	11.8
1978	1,393	1,823	430	13.2	3.60	1,823	430	13.2	3.60	1,823	430	13.2
1979	1,702	2,034	332	14.5	3.60	2,034	332	14.5	3.60	2,034	332	14.5
1980	2,034	2,242	208	15.8	3.60	2,242	208	15.8	3.60	2,242	208	15.8
1981	2,362	2,478	116	17.1	3.60	2,478	116	17.1	3.60	2,478	116	17.1
1982	2,714	2,725	11	18.3	3.60	2,725	11	18.3	3.60	2,725	11	18.3
1983	3,094	2,983	-111	19.5	3.73	3,094	0	19.6	3.60	2,983	-111	19.5
1984	3,502	3,248	-254	20.7	3.88	3,502	0	21.0	3.60	3,248	-254	20.7
1985	3,944	3,520	-424	21.8	4.03	3,944	0	22.5	3.60	3,520	-424	21.8
1990	6,750	4,925	-1,826	23.9	4.93	6,750	0	31.6	3.79	5,189	-1,562	24.0
1995	10,534	6,816	-3,718	16.7	5.56	10,534	0	43.8	4.74	8,972	-1,562	24.0
2000	15,460	9,540	-5,920	-5.5	5.83	15,460	0	60.2	5.24	13,898	-1,562	24.0
2005	21,972	13,419	-8,553	-50.0	5.89	21,972	0	82.5	5.48	20,411	-1,562	24.0
2010	31,426	18,676	-12,750	-130.4	6.06	31,426	0	113.1	5.76	29,864	-1,562	24.0
2015	46,696	25,523	-21,173	-277.6	6.59	46,696	0	155.0	6.37	45,134	-1,562	24.0
2020	69,377	34,468	-34,910	-544.7	7.25	69,377	0	212.5	7.08	67,816	-1,562	24.0
2025	102,187	46,379	-55,808	-1012.7	7.93	102,187	0	291.4	7.81	100,626	-1,562	24.0

Source: Department of Insurance

88

In Fund A:

We, the policy makers in Ottawa, freeze onto the present 3.6% contribution (tax) rate like grim death. Nothing ever convinces us that it is really insufficient. For a time, we seem to be right. The reserve fund builds steadily, the provinces bask in the sunshine of more and more cheap borrowed money, no interest is paid, and all benefit cheques go out on time.

But then, gradually, things seem to change. Even though the tax inflow is well maintained, and rises through $3 billion annually, soon after the end of 1983, those swelling benefit outflows keep on rising and rising, and have just gone ahead of our tax revenues. Our relations with the provinces have been a bit strained lately. Not only has our regular remittance money to them been shrinking for years. It has in the last year entirely dried up. Not only that, but we were forced, politely of course, to ask them for some interest on that $19 billion of ours that they were sitting on. Not very much interest, but just enough to top off our tax revenues so that all benefits could be paid.

It is now 1995. We seem to be in very big trouble, and so do the provinces. There is chaos in the money market in Toronto. It was back in 1990 that the amount in our fund topped out at $23.9 billion. With a benefit flow of $6.75 billion in that year alone, but only $4.93 billion of taxes coming in, we had to ask the provinces to pay all the interest to us that they owed us for that year. They didn't like that. Not only that, but we had to begin calling the very first of those 20-year callable bonds. That hurt even more. They had to go out and borrow on the open market just to meet our demands, in addition to their other borrowing.

But that was only the beginning. Each year since then the benefit flow has seemed to skyrocket so much faster that all previous increases seemed small. The actuaries say that still worse is to come. This seems hard to believe, because the Prime Minister is just as determined as ever to hold, and on no account to increase the 3.6% tax rate, especially with the next election coming up. After all, the fund still has $16.7 billion in it. But this constant heavy liquidation of provincial bonds and reborrowing by the provinces in the open market is causing an awful uproar in the money markets.

The year 2000 is now here. Only seems like yesterday that we had a fund. Now instead we are deep in debt. We are paying out benefit cheques every month with borrowed money. It was great that the provinces came through and loaned us the money! They had to raise their provincial tax rates and further increase their borrowing on the open market, but after all we had helped them earlier with their financial needs. Now we owe them $5.5 billion. We just don't know where it can come from.

You wouldn't believe it! Last year (2010) we paid out $31.43 billion in pension and benefit cheques. Our tax revenues were only $18.68 billion. So where did we get the rest of the money? Where we have always got it. From the provinces. In the interprovincial treasurers' conference held in the year 2005 (the press called it the Good Samaritan conference), Ontario said that it had always wanted to make a contribution to the funding of the CPP, and that the other provinces should keep in mind that the basic purpose of the CPP is to provide benefits, not provincial revenues. On the motion of Ontario, the provinces unanimously agreed that, since the CPP really belonged to them, they had a deep moral obligation to see it through its time of difficulty even though provincial taxes will again have to be doubled.

The only trouble is that the actuaries tell us that the $130.4 billion we already owe the provinces won't be enough. They even say it will be more than *$500 billion* before the next 10 years have passed, and *$1,000 billion* (a trillion) five years after that. We just wish we had a government that was able to stay in office long enough to deal with this problem. Even the provincial governments seem to be falling all the time. There seems to be some trouble among the workers and taxpayers all over the provinces. Our foreign owners are upset, too. Only the pensioners seem to be satisfied. It seems as if something big went off the track away back in time.

Is there something unreal or unnecessarily hilarious about the foregoing scenario? Not at all. Every date and figure is taken directly from the projections dated April 1976, prepared by the actuarial staff of the Department of Insurance in Ottawa. Everything else stated is implied in, or consistent with, or can very easily be imagined in the context of the Fund A projection. (This is the projection which underlies Chart XIII on page 45.) But is this a real alternative? Of course it is not. Then why bother about it? Because it shows quite graphically the direction in which the present system is already going, and how and when it will get into trouble if simply left alone.

In Fund B:

The same pleasant story unfolds as far as the year 1983. The fund builds steadily, the provinces receive funds but do not pay any interest, and benefits are paid out.

But in 1983 as in the previous projection, the moment of truth comes. Tax revenues can no longer pay the swelling benefit costs. The provinces take the position that funds loaned to them in the past are "nothing more than the sum of money that did not have to come from the provincial taxation system." It is their money to keep. The CPP did not need it when it was contributed through the 3.6% tax rate. All the interest on it has always been borrowed back by the provinces. Why should this not continue? After all the fund is nothing more than a bookkeeping fiction. The plan really belongs to the provinces, and the decision as to its method of funding "is one that must be made by the provinces participating in the plan." If the 3.6% tax rate is no longer sufficient to pay the benefits, then raise it.

So it was that in 1983 the tax rate was fixed at 3.73%; not much of an increase. But the next year it rose again, and the next year after that, and the next and the next and the next. By 1995, which came around very fast, it was up to 5.56% of pay and still rising. Meantime the fund, all invested in provincial bonds, had grown, even at substandard interest rates, to $43.8 billion. People were asking what the fund was for. They did not seem to realize that this was where the strength of the whole plan lay. The function of the fund, like any pension fund, was to make sure that benefit obligations are covered by assets. At least, this is the normal situation.

But the acid test of this came in the year 2010. Unemployment really shot up that year when the huge Consolidated Motors combine decided to pull out of Canada, and many of its local suppliers went out of business and a general wave of pessimism and layoffs swept through industry. The tax rate, which had been fixed at 6.06% for that year, simply did not yield anywhere near enough money to pay the $31.43 billion costs, which did not shrink at all even in a depression. So we had to ask the provinces to put up the difference out of the $113.1 billion fund they were holding. Did they come through? Not at all! They said that the depression was hurting them too, and besides the real purpose of the CPP was to finance them in a time of trouble, and not vice versa. You wouldn't believe the problems we had in getting the money to keep the pensions paid.

It is now the year 2025. The tax rate is going up faster and faster every year now. It was 7.93% this year, but the numbers of pensioners have been growing so fast these last few years that we are paying out $102.2 billion this year as against $69.4 billion only five years ago. The general income and other tax rates are all going up, too, to pay for the fully indexed OAS benefits to all the growing hordes of these same pensioners. There is no fund at all for these benefits. The taxpayers are getting angry. It is now 33 years since we paid anything to the provinces. When we stopped sending money to them, they owed us $18.3 billion, but the compound interest on that amount (which they never pay) has caused this to grow to $291.4 billion! They have never paid us anything at all, and say they never will. Sorry we can't say more now. We have to work on the wording of an order-in-council to raise the CPP tax rate still further.

The key to the foregoing Fund B projection is the non-payment of interest by the provinces at the time when the excess cash flow to them has stopped and money is needed by the CPP to pay benefits. But it also raises other questions. For whose benefit was the C/QPP system set up in the first place? Was it to finance the provinces and become a substitute for their own normal inflow of provincial borrowing and taxation? Not if you were there when it all happened. Not if you read Hansard. But in reading some of the statements in an official Ontario document titled "Financing the Canada Pension Plan," one gathers the strong impression that some key people in the province of Ontario have been developing this idea.

It is one thing to appear to pay a low rate of interest. It is another to *not* pay the interest at all, but to reborrow the interest. It is still another to keep putting off the payment of either capital or interest until an endless series of tomorrows that eventually fade away into the blue haze of eternity. Regardless of the book-keeping, and the apparent compounding of the debt into infinity, there are other names for this kind of an operation—names like expropriation, hijacking or just plain default. This was the kind of financing that France was doing in the period before the Revolution, and that the City of New York was doing before it ran into serious financial difficulty—issuing bonds to raise money for current expenses, and then more bonds to pay the interest on the bonds. So we can sum up the real outcome of Fund A in one word: *Collapse*. And we can sum up the real character of Fund B in another word: *Default*. Neither of these should be acceptable to the people of Canada as a proper way to pay for the costs of their CPP. Perhaps neither was ever meant to be taken seriously. So what of the third contestant?

In Fund C:

The story again unfolds pleasantly until the year 1983, when benefit payments outstrip tax inflows by $111 million.

In this scenario, the provinces shape up to their obligations like any other good borrowers and pay such interest as is needed for the basic purposes of the CPP, reborrowing only such interest as is available after the obligations of the plan to its members have been met. Each year the pension roll grows and there is less and less of this "unused" interest available, since more and more goes into benefit payments.

By the year 1990, not only is all of the available interest going into benefit payments, but the 3.6% tax rate has to be raised also. One thing that this does is to stop the growth of the fund, so that it remains thereafter as an interest-paying investment of the CPP of $24 billion.

The provinces have done very well out of this. They have had a nice steady source of capital made available to them at cheap rates for many years, but in the end, like any other borrower, they have to start paying interest on their bonds. To do this, they have had to raise provincial taxes and find other sources for their borrowing. In any normal pension funding situation, the CPP could theoretically call all the bonds and do a much better job of investing its assets, as Quebec has done. But since any drastic move in this direction would cause havoc in the capital markets, the provinces are left with this capital in their treasuries and are not asked for repayment, even though the interest rate is low.

It is now the year 2010, the year of heavy unemployment. The 5.76% tax rate was supposed to bring in $29.86 billion this year, but due to the number of people out of work, only $27 billion can be expected. The interest payments from the provinces ($1.56 billion) help, but desperate measures are still needed to raise enough money to meet the growing commitments to pensioners, which never shrink but only grow. Times are very hard. Only the pensioners are protected against all of these problems, and have nothing to worry about.

As 2025 dawns, the flood of pensions seems to be swamping everything. The 7.81% tax rate will bring in $100.63 billion this year. Adding the $1.56 billion of interest from the provinces on the $24-billion fund they still have, we can gather up enough revenue to cover the $102.2-billion benefit outflow expected for the year.

We still have two terrifying problems, however:

1. The thundering increase each year in the pensioner rolls. This is affecting OAS costs, and the taxes to pay for these too.

2. The vulnerability of the nation to a catastrophic financial crisis in paying for benefits of this size if we have another recession year like the one we had in 2010 or, prior to that, in the 1975-76 period.

So if the real name of Fund A is Collapse, and Fund B is Default, how should we regard Fund C? At least it is honest. The terrifying prospect at the end is common to all systems of paying for these indexed benefits, commencing at age 65, regardless of the realities of the times. The underlying cause is demographic. Nothing we can do will stop the inexorable surge of people into the older age groups at about the time we have described.

But unlike Funds A and B, the problems that arise in Fund C are not due to a failure to adjust the 3.6% tax rate (as in Fund A) or a total misconstruction of the purposes of the plan, resulting in

94

$24 billion of CPP taxpayers' money being coolly expropriated by the provinces (as in Fund B).

Does this mean that Fund C is the choice that Canadians should select? Not necessarily. It is certainly preferable to Funds A and B which should both be dropped from all future actuarial studies in Ottawa. But Fund C, as it has been projected, leaves the CPP exposed to the possibility of a short-term liquidity crisis in the event of a depression.

In our scenario we presented only one such depression. There could of course be more, and there could also be other kinds of changes. Are we sure that $24 billion in "callable" 20-year provincial bonds would really be liquid enough, as time goes on, and as the fantastic growth in pension rolls occurs in the early part of the next century? Are the provinces really the best source of huge volumes of money at short notice in the event of a sudden unforeseen economic downturn? Perhaps a better answer would be Fund C together with a cushion fund that is both (a) really liquid, and (b) in an amount that is related to the growing size of the pension roll. But why $24 billion? If these provincial bonds are not yielding a very good return, and not really helping to increase the GNP very much, why continue their growth from $9 billion to $24 billion? Why not blow the whistle?

The Ontario brief

Section 115(4) of the Canada Pension Plan Act provides that changes in the CPP cannot be made except with the consent of at least two thirds of the participating provinces containing at least two thirds of the population. This places Ontario, which has one half of the population outside Quebec in the special position of being able to block anything it does not like. It also places a special responsibility on Ontario to be well informed as to both the broader and the more technical aspects of CPP matters, and to act in an enlightened manner.

In these circumstances it is startling to see a document titled "Financing the Canada Pension Plan" bearing the proud heraldry of the Province of Ontario, dated April 1976, signed by Hon. W. Darcy McKeough, Provincial Treasurer and Minister of Economics, and by A. Rendall Dick, QC, his Deputy Minister. The document is complete with charts, tables, and enough symbolic notation in the appendix to confuse most readers. It throws actuarial and pseudo-actuarial terminology around like a drunken technician, but obviously is written by a person who is no actuary at all and who does not understand the normal procedures involved in financing pensions. Destined to be enshrined in history as a document containing the most elementary howlers, or to become a collectors' item like a postage stamp with the Queen's head printed upside down, this document, interweaving technology with error, includes these gems:

—"There is one common feature of the fully funded, partially funded and paygo financial structures. In the long run they all tend to converge to the same contribution rate, known as the equilibrium contribution rate." (This is followed by a graph which shows that the author actually believes what he has just said.)

—"In the long run, the same equilibrium is needed as with a fully funded method, the only difference being in the accumulation of a large fund. Interest is not used for financing benefits."

—"The previous funding methods are conventional in terms of actuarial methods of funding."

It need hardly be stated here that in a normally funded pension plan the interest and other investment yield generated by fund assets make an important contribution toward reducing contributions and paying benefits.

There is a matter of professional ethics involved here. The Canadian Institute of Actuaries has procedures for dealing with or disciplining those of its members whose work or conduct do not meet proper standards. How should the institute deal with a province that employs professionally qualified actuaries on its staff, but nevertheless produces this kind of nonsense without asking for their help?

But there are other aspects of this that should concern Canadians:

1. The non-payment of interest until now by the provinces on the money borrowed from the CPP seems to have cast such a hypnotic spell over the thinking that underlies this brief that the very possibility that the CPP would ever use or have access to the interest on its own investments to pay benefits to its members is never even contemplated.

Highly confused and erroneous statements are instead put forward to the effect that in an actuarially funded plan, interest is not used to finance benefits. How would Canadians feel about the control of their nation-wide plan being governed by this kind of thinking?

2. If this is a reflection of Ontario's competence in these matters, does this not show up a serious structural weakness in the way the CPP is set up? Where is the full-time chief actuary or actuarial staff, or the free-standing board of actuaries—like the one which fearlessly stated the facts about the burgeoning costs under the U.S. civil service retirement system quoted earlier—which could represent the interests and concerns of the CPP and the millions of Canadians whose money and security are tied up in it?

There are no insurance companies with $9 billion of assets that feel they can limp along on a little time borrowed from the chief actuary of the Department of Insurance.

3. If the borrowing of money at cheap rates from the CPP is of great assistance to provincial treasurers, are not the provinces in a position of conflict of interest in trying to deal impartially with CPP funding policy questions? Can Canada afford to see its CPP become the victim of that conflict of interest? With its veto power under present law, is not the Province of Ontario especially exposed to this problem?

4. Apart from the inadequacy of its central actuarial facilities, is there not a great structural weakness in the method of control and direction or application of the funds becoming available for investment? Why is there no proper evidence as to exactly how the investment of this fund has strengthened the sinews of the Canadian economy and made it more able to provide the benefits in due course to those whose contributions have gone into it?

One is reminded of Parkinson's second law, which states that expenditures always rise to meet revenue. By making these funds automatically available to the provinces, are we not simply inviting extravagance in provincial expenditures with nothing very much to show at the end? Is this the best use that Canada can make of $15 billion more of these funds? (This is the difference between the present and ultimate projection C funds.)

5. The lack of integrity of the C/QPP, its dismemberment as a matter of theory and to some extent as a matter of fact, and par-

celling out the money among the provinces.

When the U.S. Social Security system was established, this same problem was faced at the outset. "In proposing a national compulsory system, the staff sought to controvert the most rigid precedent in our legal system, the separation of functions of the federal and state governments," states J. Douglas Brown, now a professor emeritus at Princeton University, who was chairman of the committee which faced and overcame this constitutional problem and went on to design the Social Security system.

Is it impossible for Canada similarly to get its basic nationwide earnings-based pension system all under one roof? Pension systems of this kind are not improved by being fragmented.

". . . We find ourselves in the position that we are in today, with critical financing questions to be answered and no underlying philosophy for guidance . . . We must commence discussions on alternatives for financing the CPP as soon as possible. I suggest that we convene a future meeting of this group to deal exclusively with this problem." So stated Hon. W. Darcy McKeough of Ontario in his much improved statement to the provincial ministers of finance in October 1976.

There is of course need for discussion. We must see that, apart from the provincial finance ministers, who have a common interest involved, the public at large is adequately represented in these discussions. It is their money at stake.

Seeing it whole

When it comes to pensions, Canada has a knack of splitting the subject matter into two parts, throwing one part in the trash can, and doing a great deal of work on the other part. How else can one explain elaborate CPP benefit and cost projections, but nowhere find any calculations or projections of the total national pension liabilities or annual costs, which all have to be borne at the same time essentially by the same taxpayers, including C/QPP, OAS/GIS and all similar pension costs? How else can one explain the otherwise highly competent actuarial valuation of the public service retirement system which diligently excludes all that large portion of the cost that will result from inflation and fall upon the general taxpayer? From this propensity for dichotomy

98

comes bad policy. If those who have to make decisions cannot see the whole picture, how can good decisions be made?

In this context we have been bombarded with proposals to expand the CPP that fail to recognize the OAS, the costs, the private plans, the economy and the next generation. We can plunge the nation into a vast program of unknown costs for benefits of unestablished need, but do nothing at all to strengthen the economy to provide these expanded benefits, and say of this afterward: "Though the financial implications of these changes were recognized, they were considered of secondary importance compared to the social objectives that were being achieved."

We can say of the CPP that in return for contributing a little for a short time to the cost of pensions for today's older people, the present generation acquires a *right* to a pension of far, far greater value, which imposes an *obligation* on the next generation to meet its cost. And in saying this, we can leave unanswered the question of inter-generational equity—that is, not asking the next generation to pay a higher rate of taxes than we ourselves are prepared to pay.

We go to great lengths to sacrifice everything for the education and comfort of our children, while entrapping them in an automatically indexed device that will squeeze the pips out of them later. We talk blandly about "an implied social contract" between the generations, but there is no evidence that the next generation (today's children and the unborn) has expressed consent. Innocent of its awful implications they need their advocates at the councils of today to forestall their economic strangulation at our hands. Having enmeshed them, we rely wholly on them, and proceed in blind faith.

We speak of contributions, and tell today's employee to write down his earnings up to the Yearly Maximum Pensionable Earnings (YMPE), deduct the Yearly Basic Exemption (YBE), multiply by nine, double (or quadruple) it, cross off the last figure and divide by 100. "The answer you get will be your annual contribution," we tell him in official CPP booklets, and he does this arithmetic and pays his contribution and thinks he is accumulating something real, and that his rights to benefits are backed up by these contributions and those of the employer. But we do not tell him that this is not so. We do not tell him that in the end, after he has paid a lifetime of these contributions, there will be nothing more to support his benefits than his children's and some other children's willingness and ability to pay taxes.

And so it is entirely understandable that in the minds of many earnest politicians and social workers and labor leaders who have the natural desire to do much good for many people today, it seems logical to select the pathway that now promises the most benefits in the future while creating the least cost now. Thus they turn to the CPP as the vehicle that seems to be capable of providing more security, more presently committed future benefits, more prospects of freedom from want, at less cost now, than anything else one can think of.

Left in the shadows is the question of committing the earnings of the next generation without their knowledge or protest, and the great truth that cost not met today will not vanish but will come back and haunt our tomorrow. There are some who would say that all of this promise of large benefits for the multitudes of tomorrow has to be an illusion, and others that it is a fraud on the next generation.

The great dilemma

A logician, on reflecting about all this, would after a time be inclined like Archimedes to cry "Eureka!", leap out of his bathtub, and rush out into print, advocating:

1. A uniform level tax rate that would be sufficient to fund the CPP throughout the next three generations, without any further increase in the rate being necessary, notwithstanding the demographic tidal wave ahead.

2. The investment of the enormous fund that would result from all of this in things that boost productivity, increase the GNP, make foreign borrowing unnecessary, build Mackenzie Valley pipelines, solar power installations, dissolve all the oil out of those tar sands, probe for hidden minerals in every corner of Canada, and set up plants to process this new wealth and convert it into consumer goods and material comforts.

Here at least would be an approach that would meet the criteria of inter-generational equity, increased productivity, fiscal responsibility, economic sense, actuarial soundness and national independence. The tax rate would be higher than 3.6% and the provinces would have to look elsewhere for money, but with the new strong well-capitalized economy, that money would be available in the newly booming capital markets.

So why not do it?

One country did do it. Sweden built up a single, centralized, gigantic, monolithic pension fund that in time dwarfed all other institutions and all other economic enterprise. By owning or controlling everything of any size or importance in Sweden, it sat and sits like a giant octopus with its tentacles penetrating every nook and cranny of the country. To get control of it has become the aim of each political party and contending faction. Is this what we want?

The whole purpose and justification of prefunding pensions on an actuarial basis springs from:

—A need to provide the capability to make payments when due.

—A desire to spread out into an even flow of costs the foreseeable heavy increase in the burden of payments being committed.

—A substantial reduction in the ultimate cost burden through the generation of investment earnings by the reserve fund set up to achieve these purposes.

Private pension funds do meet these tests, and are helpful to the economy. Public systems such as the OAS and the CPP, because of their *lack* of actuarial funding, have a totally different impact on the economy.

To put the public plans on a similarly funded centrally controlled basis would involve the establishment of reserves many times as great as the present C/QPP reserves, and create the problem of overconcentration of economic might in one place. It could also lead to:

1. An early miscarriage of the basic intent of the funding program through political interference, such as diversion of funds into nonproductive or "social" (present-consumption) uses; and/or

2. A further expansion or proliferation of benefits as the fund begins to grow, largely cancelling out the effects of the funding program. "I just do not trust congressional use of the funds for

capital formation . . . As the reserve fund increases they will be tempted to pay out larger benefits," stated a well-known American research economist with long experience in government policy problems. The same would apply in Canada.

Reluctantly, then, we have to turn away from this seemingly logical solution to the whole problem, realizing in doing so that passions and politics, the bottomless well of human wants and eversprouting lust for power, are hazards and forces that have to be reckoned with no less than productivity, interest rates, inflation and demography. It does seem a shame that a nation cannot manage its own social security system without having to be driven up the wall by it in one way or another. To make economic sense, it would have to become an untamable political monstrosity. Keeping it politically docile requires its economic emasculation so that from the viewpoint of the economy it tends to become a functionless burden. With these inherent problems, should we then be further expanding these public plans?

Is there no better way of providing for our later years? Can we not have both benefits that are adequate, and funds that are adequate and productively invested, with neither getting out of control?

To these questions we shall have several answers. But first, let us look briefly at what has been done recently to the CPP, and what further changes are proposed.

Recent changes

Since the CPP's inception only 10 years ago, sweeping liberalizations have been made in its benefit structure, adding to ultimate benefit costs. Some of these have been necessary to keep the plan up-to-date in an inflationary economy; some have done more than this.

—The old 2% ceiling on pension increases, intended to offset inflation, has been blown out, and presently there is no limit.

—The YMPE is calculated by a new expanding formula.

—The retirement and earnings tests have been repealed, so that pensions are payable at age 65 even though full-time work continues. The pension thus becomes an *added* layer of income.

—Spouses and survivors of disabled or deceased female tax-

102

payers now get benefits without proving dependency.

All of these in combination have added greatly to the amount, the availability, and the value of benefits provided by the CPP.

With all of this, there has been no change at all in the 3.6% tax rate. Nor does any contributor today, no matter how old or young, pay for anything like the actuarial value of the benefits he can expect to receive.

This is intoxicating stuff for any politician or social worker. Here is a system that seems to have a magic capacity to get more and more benefits out of the hat with nothing more at all going into it. The only apparent effect is that those dry figures on the sheet of paper with Funds A, B and C on it have changed a bit. The tax rates that the next generation will have to pay have just gone up by 1% of its gross earnings as a result of this last round of changes alone, but this need not concern present taxpayers. Think of all the human wants and needs that can be satisfied now in this way. So why not let us have some more of this joy juice? It is an irresistable formula.

Proposals for change

Into this situation comes Martin O'Connell, MP, who has worked up his own proposal to solve most of Canada's retirement problems by:

—Doubling the benefits under the C/QPP, over a period;

—Leaving the 3.6% tax rate alone, at least until 1985;

—Not disturbing the OAS, except to provide it with a minimum level.

Revealing his proposal by removing one veil at a time, Martin O'Connell pushes hardest for the first stage of his plan, which would only add 60% to present benefit levels, raising the present 25% of pay to 40% of pay, over and above both private and OAS benefits. He carefully points out the modesty of the costs of his proposal by emphasizing the thin end of the wedge, and the cost increment, which he ambiguously describes as though it covers the whole of his 40% formula, attributing the quoted figures to official sources.

"One can attribute to the 40% formula itself, standing apart from other factors, a cost reflected in the combined [employer plus employee] rate of 1.6% by 1985, 3.5% by the year 2000, and 4.6% by the year 2025," he states.

One cannot believe that a statement as misleading as this, or as careless at the very least, could have been intentional. At least its context, if studied carefully, makes it clear that even he did not mean what he said.

But Martin O'Connell has other things in mind for the CPP. He has looked into its funding and studied Funds A, B and C. After concluding that Fund B means that provincial governments would never repay their debts, but would be going ever deeper into debt, and that "in this respect it might be argued that [CPP tax] rates included an element of provincial taxation," he turns to Fund C.

It will be remembered that under Fund C, the provinces are called on to start paying interest on their borrowings when the total benefit needs of the CPP first exceed tax revenues, and that the fund tops out at $24 billion, and is thereafter frozen and interest-bearing. Under Martin O'Connell's approach, the provincial treasurers all get a nice big bonus. The $24 billion debt is permitted to grow by 60%, just like the benefits, so that interest payments will not have to start for quite some time after all. But there is more. With all that extra provincial debt being created, perhaps the private sector should get a break, too. So "up to 50% of the increased reserves [sic] related to the 40% proposal should be channeled through an independent agency or agencies into the private sector of the economy in response to the very heavy capital needs of the private sector over the next two decades. Distribution of investments should no doubt be by province in accordance with receipts."

So everybody is given to believe that he will get a prize. It is just like starting a whole new layer of the CPP, as to benefits but not as to costs. For the next 10 years, the costs are not increased at all. The 3.6% tax rate stays unchanged. Even though the benefits are increased, and the taxes are not increased (yet), the provinces can look forward to going joyously a good deal further into debt to the CPP than they can at present, while private industry is at the same time replenished with capital (how, it is not clear), and all workers can at the same time look forward happily to larger pensions than they ever thought they could receive.

104

All is rapture. Or is it?

There are some grim truths in this that need to be stated. First, we have to look at the impact of these proposals on the amount of benefits that would be provided by the public plans. Then we have to see how private employers would respond to the new situation. From there we have to follow the chain reaction into the capital markets and the economy as a whole. Finally, we have to study the position in which we would be placing future generations.

As to benefit levels

In his address before the "Pensions in Crisis" conference in Toronto on September 16, 1975, Health and Welfare Minister Marc Lalonde made these points about the present size of tax-supported pensions in Canada:

1. Whereas in 1965 an elderly couple was assured of a public pension of *$1,800 a year*, commencing at *age 70*, by October 1975 the amounts under OAS/GIS alone had grown to more than *$5,000 a year*, commencing at *age 65*.

2. In the case of a single-wage-earner family, with gross earnings of $10,000 a year (about the average industrial wage), living in Ontario, and reaching retirement age, along with the spouse, in January 1976, the net take-home pay for 1975, after taxes and CPP, UIC and Ontario Health Insurance Plan deductions, would be about *$8,300 a year*.

3. What could this same couple expect to receive from the government in 1976, the first retirement year? According to the Minister, they could expect *$6,700 a year* from the CPP, OAS/GIS and Ontario tax-credit programs alone. Their net income would thus be *more than 80%* of their pre-retirement net income. And this leaves out of account:

—Any income from private pension plans, RRSP's, savings, investments, etc.

—The savings due to the elimination of work-related costs such as the cost of commuting to work each day, union dues, etc.

—The wide range of free services and discounts available to retired people.

When it is recognized, further, that this 80% is fully indexed, without limit, for all the rest of their lives, *where is the justification* for a 60% or 100% increase in the CPP portion?

As to private pension plans

The role of these plans was narrowed by the establishment of the CPP at a time, 10 years ago, when the pension movement as a whole was at an earlier stage in its development, and benefit levels had not reached anywhere near a saturation point. The situation today is different. Successive liberalizations of both public and private plans have already advanced to the point where the combined level of retirement incomes from all sources is increasingly often higher than was the net take-home pay from full-time work. In the case described by Lalonde, it would take only a very modest and below-average amount of private pension to create this situation, without considering any of the other factors.

It is also true that private employers, to be successful, have to be careful about what they do with money. If it is simply being wasted, the source of waste must be eliminated. If it is being spent for unnecessary luxuries, these too must be cut back or eliminated.

Imagine the situation, then, of a private employer, concerned for the welfare of his employees, but faced with the government pensions and prospective costs that would exist if proposals such as those of Martin O'Connell were given effect. How could such an employer do otherwise than cut back or terminate the pension plan covering these employees or simply omit to establish a pension plan for them? The mere automatic action of many integration formulas would cut back the pensions prior to retirement under many pension plans in any case; or if they did not, they would soon have to be adjusted to do this. After all, pension plans are not and never were intended to create and enrich a whole new generation of privileged persons living at substantially higher standards of income and expenditure than those who are coping with the strains and pressures of full-time work. Neither cost nor common sense nor the social conscience would long remain indifferent to unjustifiable, unbalanced privilege and extravagance of this kind.

We cannot therefore in any way accept Martin O'Connell's

106

opinion when, in presenting his proposals at the May 4, 1976, convention of the Canadian Pension Conference, he made reference to the probable effect of his 40% formula on the private plans by comparing this to the first introduction of the C/QPP, which slowed but did not stop the growth of these private plans, stating: "It would not, in my view, reverse their growth trend."

If your young son is four feet tall, and you stand him in water three feet deep, he will stay alive and even keep on growing. But if you increase the depth of the water by 60%, or double it, something entirely different will happen. This is a good parallel to what Martin O'Connell is proposing.

When the Canada Pension Plan was established, there was a greater vacuum for retirement benefits than exists today. Some employee groups were well provided for, but many were not. In the 10 years of its existence, the process of filling this vacuum has continued both through the continued growth of private plans and also through liberalization of the public plans. The establishment of the C/QPP did, however, slow down the growth of the private plans. In its publication "Pension Plans in Canada: 1974", Statistics Canada described this as follows:

"The sharply increasing growth . . .[of] pension plans in the 1950s and early 1960s reached its peak by the mid-1960s and then in the early 1970s levelled off or fell back somewhat. The dampened growth rate, particularly over the last half of the 1960s was attributable to some degree at least, to the introduction of the C/QPP . . . The new public programme had wide-ranging effects on existing occupational schemes. Some plans were cancelled outright, though these were limited to relatively small plans with comparatively low benefits, while in others some participants cancelled membership, withdrew their accumulated contributions and chose to rely entirely on the C/QPP . . .

"Thus pension plans which had grown to 8,920 in number by 1960 increased by over 50% by 1965; . . . by 1970 growth dropped sharply to 18% . . . and then ceased entirely . . . with a decline of slightly under 2% in 1974."

Even though the number of employees covered, and the dollar amounts of covered payrolls and fund assets have continued to grow, reflecting inflation and normal growth, the stage has been reached now where a further wide-scale expansion of the CPP would inevitably cause a retraction of the private plans. This would mean a choking off of the infusion of new capital into the economy from the diversified, and hence politically benign, private pension funds. This, as we have seen earlier, would have devastating effects on the economy.

These damaging effects would not await the slow, advancing tide of taxation set in motion by these proposals and destined gradually to inundate a rising generation already burdened down with their demographic legacy. Not at all. Pension plans are funded with an eye to the long future. If it ever became established that the CPP were to expand its benefit levels, even though this expansion would be staged over a period of many years, then the design and prefunding of benefits under private plans would promptly respond to the changed future outlook for nonfunded public pensions, and the flow of new moneys into the capital markets to provide for future private pensions would drop, and the life and momentum of the economy would die down.

The sickly, inflation-ridden economies of Britain and Italy provide us with present-day examples of what the economy of Canada could easily become, given enough of this combination of capital starvation and rising pension and welfare taxation. At a seven-country economic summit conference held in Puerto Rico in 1976, former U.S. President Gerald Ford delivered a stern warning to Britain and Italy in particular to get their social welfare costs under control as a first step toward strengthening and stabilizing their ailing economies and faltering currencies.

The OAS/GIS and the CPP each fill a certain role in the Canadian pension picture. Around these, over the years, have grown the private plans, many of which have had to move over and be adjusted as the public plans have become established. In combination, the outcome has been good for Canadians, though improvements are possible, as we shall discuss later.

If the doubling or the 60% expansion of the CPP, as proposed by Martin O'Connell, would be damaging to the Canadian economy and the Canadian people, what then are we to conclude about the proposals advanced by the Canadian Labor Congress not to double, but to *triple* the CPP, and to have the benefit commence at age 60 rather than 65?

This CLC proposal, never formulated in detail, would carry in it the seeds of a total destruction of the whole economic base on which the Canadian people, including all of the CLC members themselves, depend. One needs only to refer back to Chart V on page 20, showing the advance in pension costs as the retirement age is lowered. Then consider the absolute devastation that a move such as this would inflict on the entire private pension movement and new capital flow, realizing that the resulting ultimate 30% CPP wage tax would drive the *total* burden of taxation far above 50% of income. One can then visualize the smoking ruins of the Canadian economy in which the members of the CLC would be picking their way while inflation like a skeleton stalked the land. The Canadian dollar has lost a great deal of its purchasing power in these last 10 years. This would finish it.

CHAPTER SIX

What We Must All Do

"The Congress finds that the growth in size, scope, and numbers of employee benefit plans in recent years has been rapid and substantial; that the operational scope and economic impact of such plans is increasingly interstate; that the continued well-being and security of millions of employees and their dependents are directly affected by these plans; that they are affected with a national public interest; that they have become an important factor affecting the stability of employment and the successful development of industrial relations . . ."

Introduction to the
U.S. Employee Retirement Income Security Act of 1974

Fifteen or 20 years ago it used to be said that the national sport in Canada was to sit on the border and criticize the way things were done in the United States. But in recent years a new game has captured the national attention—criticizing the private pension systems.

And so we have been bombarded with headlines telling us that the coverage of pension plans is hit-and-miss, that the average investment yield of pension funds is below average, that you may never receive your pension, that pensions are being ruined by inflation, that they unfairly exclude housewives. "Can private pension plans deliver?" provocatively demands the catchy title of one article, while others mock back: "Muddled pension picture means poverty"—"Pension liabilities dampen profits"—"The private pension system doesn't work."

Just as, when products compete with one another, they improve as if by a magic process, so also there are some strong growing things that positively flourish on criticism, and improve as a result of it. The private pension movement seems to be one of these. For example, during the past 15 years:

—The membership in private pension plans has doubled.
—The contribution income has quintupled.
—The assets held have quintupled.
—Pension outflows have increased *sevenfold.*
—Their contribution to capital formation has quintupled.

In the four years 1972-5, one can watch quarter-by-quarter the steady increase in pension payments and in assets of trusteed plans as these rise without interruption:

	1972 First Quarter	1975 Last Quarter
	$ million	
Pensions paid out (annualized)	544	884
Reserves: Bonds (book value)	6,669	10,059
Stocks (book value)	3,328	5,232
Mortgages	1,212	2,373
Total (above plus miscellaneous)	12,799	20,954

In other words, the contribution of the private plans both to the security of workers and to the strength of the economy have been vast and beneficial. Why, then, has there been all the outcry?

There are three distinct reasons:
1. There are some fairly basic improvements needed in the way the private plans operate, which we shall discuss herein.
2. There have been some gross misunderstandings about the

111

extent of the private plans' coverage and their contribution to the wellbeing of the nation.

3. The private plans did not get started early enough to enable many workers who are now retired and at high ages to receive adequate pensions. This is something that time is correcting.

We are understandably impatient for improvements. It is no bad thing to have all this criticism and sensationalism, so long as we do not lose our perspectives. But at least we should get our facts straight.

The shocks and myths of pension uncoverage

In its polemic about retirement policies in Canada released in November 1975, the Canadian Council on Social Development, not having access at the time to statistics later than 1970, states:

"In 1960, 34% of paid workers were in group pension plans. In 1965, 35% were covered and, in 1970, 39% . . . Even if in the ensuing four years a further half million people have been enrolled . . . the proportion will have remained *well below the 40% mark.*"

In his brief "Pensions in Canada: Proposals for Change," dated June 1975, Martin O'Connell stated:

"In the post-war period they [private pension plans] grew rapidly, yet by 1965 covered only 38% of the paid employees in the work force . . . By 1970, the private plans covered 39% of paid workers. This proportion grew to *40%* by June 1, 1974. Thus a major weakness in private pensions is that 60% of workers are not covered. When public service and Crown corporation employees are subtracted from the total, it becomes clear that only some 25%-30% of paid employees in private corporations are covered by pension plans and some 70%-75% are not covered."

It is from figures like these that much of the argument has come for expanding the CPP. If private employers are not providing coverage for their employees, there is a vacuum, so the argument runs, and this must therefore be filled by the CPP. A sad situation. *But is it real?*

After the heat and the shock effect of this approach had been created, and much damage had been done, there came in due course the cold light of the next morning, and with it a totally different perspective. For example, of the total labor force in 1973:

112

—5.7% were aged 14-19.
—3.7% were non-paid family workers, or over 65.
—9.6% were part-time workers only.
—9.0% were self-employed.
—13.4% were aged 20-24.
—5.6% were unemployed.

Thus 47% of the labor force were not exactly in the mainstream, and if you compare the 40% who were covered (it is now 41%) with the remaining 53%, the answer comes out at 75%, not 40%. This is quite a different story. Note also that:

1. Many not now covered *will soon become covered* simply by continuing to work and hence to qualify for eligibility to be covered.

2. Many not now covered have *elected* not to be covered.

3. The 1.2 million Canadians now covered by Registered Retirement Savings Plans are nowhere referred to in these figures. To some extent they overlap, or are among the self-employed whom we have excluded from our base figure. Their inclusion would increase the 75% figure to something higher.

Statistics Canada, using a somewhat different approach and again excluding RRSPs, has stated in its publication "Pension Plans in Canada 1974" that 60% of all paid workers were with organizations providing pensions. On October 21, 1976, Harry Weitz of Statistics Canada said in his careful address before the Canadian Pension Conference that some *62%* of "full-time employed paid workers between the ages of 25 and 64" are covered by private pension plans.

Who then are the remainder, not included in the 75% or 60% or 62%? Apart from the young, the part-time, the voluntary non-participants, the unemployed, the over-65s, there is a section of the work force that is not being reached by private pension plans. These work mainly for small businesses, for retail stores, for professional people and for small agencies and contractors. How can these workers become covered? It is important that this be done.

The highly-informed advisory committee attached to the CPP has suggested this approach: "An alternative solution to the problem would be . . . legislation requiring employers to adopt a minimum private pension plan for all employees . . . just [as] employers are now forced, through legislation, to pay minimum current wages."

This approach would avoid the cutback and disruption of existing plans that would result from an expansion of the CPP, would result in higher pensions in total, would direct the action to where it is needed, and would materially assist the economy, as explained elsewhere. *Here, then, is something we can all support.*

The strange case of the industry that vanished

A good magician can spellbind his audience by pulling rabbits out of a hat. But it takes a special kind of magician to make a whole industry disappear into a hat.

If you look at the full-page graph on page 27 of "Pension Plans in Canada: 1974", published by Statistics Canada, you will see that only 1.1% of the workers in the forestry industry are covered by any private pension plans. Table E on page 28 confirms this, and further shows that only a mere 873 of these unfortunate workers have this privileged protection. The Financial Post of March 8, 1975, in a lengthy article, "How private plans could plug major gaps," reprints an earlier version of this graph, and states "forestry workers have almost no pension plans," and helpfully suggests a solution.

And so the bad news spreads, and even the CPP's well-informed advisory committee perpetuates the misunderstanding in its report which has been laid before Parliament, stating: "To get a more accurate assessment of the coverage of private pension plans, it is important to consider specific industries separately. The proportion of paid workers participating in private pension arrangements is much below average in . . . forestry . . ."

So, in Ottawa and all across Canada, people wring their hands for the poor workers in the forest industries. Those who write polemics in favor of expanding the CPP can find no better industry to quote, and anyone who knows anything about pensions is aware of this very serious failure of private industry to care for its workers properly.

Meantime, out in Vancouver, and not exactly appreciating all this, sits Gerry Dorset, presiding over the awesome task of administering the giant IWA-Forest Industry Pension Plan, with more

114

than 70,000 covered members, and in another building sits Doreen Funk with similar responsibility for the IWA-Southern Interior Forest Pension Plan and the IWA-Northern Interior Forest Pension Plan, with another 35,000 covered members between them. So here we have more than 100,000 workers in the forest products industries covered in three gigantic industry-wide pension plans. How come? What went wrong? How did Statistics Canada find itself in the position of starting a powder train like that? Did they not have copies of those forest industry plans?

Being concerned about the dangers that lurk in graphs like that, and what these can lead to in the way of bad policy, the author took the trouble to phone Harry Weitz in Statistics Canada, Ottawa, who is very knowledgeable about pensions, and put the questions to him.

"The problem is one of classification," stated Harry Weitz. "We put each plan under only one industry classification."

Since about two thirds of the workers covered work in sawmills, plywood mills, and similar activities, and only about one third out in the forest, falling and logging, the entire plans are classified under "manufacturing." The forestry industries, completely blanketed as they are in the West, where most of the action is, by three large and lusty industry-wide pension plans, including more than 30,000 members whose work has been right out there in the forests, are thus statistically obliterated, denuded of their excellent pension coverage, while the official tabulation shows a mere 873 to be covered.

"We tried to make it clear in the text," said Harry Weitz. And if you read it all, sure enough there it is: "Difficulties arise with the large integrated companies whose operations cut across a number of industrial sectors . . . the classification of these units severely limits the validity of the industrial distribution presented in this report."

There is always a danger that policy-makers will take graphs and charts too readily at face value. Too busy in conferences and in the decision-making process itself, these highly responsible persons do not have time to check out all the possible statistical traps in the information placed before them. This is not their line of work. To develop good policy, we have to understand and to try to communicate the *realities* that lie beyond the graphs and figures.

Sometimes that is not easy. There is much misinformation in the pension field.

The RRSPs

The Cinderella of the pension movement in Canada, usually overlooked when comparisons are made between public and private provisions for retirement, the Registered Retirement Savings Plans are in fact now rising to become a comely addition to the family. While the number of persons covered by private pension plans increased by 50% in the last 10 years, the number of new RRSP registrations went up by 1,336% in only nine years:

1965	29,190
1970	76,983
1974	419,416

The Canadians who were thus making provision for own retirement were from every income class and age group. There is no age or income subgroup in which the use of this tax-sheltered approach to saving has not grown steadily throughout recent years. For example, the dollars set aside in 1970 and 1973 were as follows:

Age Group	1970	1973
	\$ million	
Under 25..	2.2	13.9
25-29	7.8	54.7
30-39	43.4	188.1
40-49	75.4	278.9
50-59	66.0	271.9
60 and over	30.4	115.1
	225.2	922.6

These figures include only amounts deducted from income for tax purposes. There may have been more. Projecting forward from 1970-73 statistics, we might get some impression of the extent of this movement, as shown in the table at the top of the opposite page.

116

	Number	Amount $ million
1970	248,719	225.2
1971	347,674	319.8
1972	545,416	645.1
1973	757,926	922.6
1974 (estimated)	980,000	1,250.0
1975 (estimated)	1,200,000	1,575.0

This money is flowing into these RRSPs from the self-employed (who can deposit 20% of their income, but not more than $5,500), from people already covered by pension plans (whose limit is $3,500 less than any contributions under these plans), from transfers from pension plans on termination or retirement, and from others.

Why have these RRSPs become so popular? It is because they are versatile, giving individual choice as to amount deposited each year, and as between bond, mortgage or equity investments—and they are 100% portable. No problems or forfeitures in the event of change of job.

Employers can assist their employees in this matter by setting up group RRSPs, which make it possible to save by payroll deduction while the employee retains full ownership rights in what is saved and set aside—with or without subsidy by the employer.

There are no problems of relationships between RRSPs and the CPP. Being fully funded, their effect is benign and helpful to the economy. In fact they are already making a handy contribution to new capital formation. *These RRSPs are something to be encouraged in every way.*

Deferred profit sharing plans now have a tax ceiling of $3,500 in place of the former $2,500. Since there is a greater hazard (and participation along with the employer in risk) in these plans, one could argue that this ceiling should be still higher.

It may surprise even most experts to know that while the private pensions are contributing a hefty $3 billion annually to the urgent investment needs of the Canadian economy, and the C/QPP a temporary and soon-faltering $2 billion, the lowly and almost unrecognized RRSPs have come surging up out of nothing and have probably already passed the $1.5-billion mark. There is

117

nothing small or insignificant about that. It is a healthy manifestation of individual desires for independence.

The great beauty of all of these plans is that they can easily reach to the *small* employer, the self-employed tradesman, the professional, the worker in the corner grocery store, the person who is not now being reached by the private pension plans of governments and large corporations. *They are very much needed, and should be even more widely used and understood.*

What the private plans must do

In a world of improving standards, and in the light of all the helpful and unhelpful criticisms that have been heaped on them, and the threats to cut them down and displace them by expanding the CPP instead, the private pension plans have some shaping up to do. Canada needs them desperately. There is no substitute for the unique role they presently occupy in the economy. They must continue to grow and to serve the many millions of workers and their dependents and survivors for whose benefit they have been established. What then are their main weaknesses, the areas where improvements are most needed? These are:

1. Transferability:
Most frequent of all criticisms, the threat of losing accruing pension rights on transfer or termination of employment urgently needs attention.

The concept of vesting the pension, which means continuing the ownership by the former employee of his right to the pension based on his service prior to termination, is no longer new in the pension field; it has become firmly established. At one time Canada seemed to be well ahead of the field, requiring all future pensions to be vested by age 45 with 10 years service. This is no longer adequate. In the United States, for example, new legislation sets three alternative minimum vesting standards, all more liberal.

It is time for Canada to recognize that its standards have become obsolete. Even these obsolete standards do not exist in all provinces. It is this obsolescence and inadequacy that have opened the way for much of the attack from those who would "solve" the problem by destroying the private plans and substitut-

118

ing the non-funded but fully transferable CPP. To survive and adequately serve those for whom they are established, the private plans must do better in this area. A first step would be to match the American standards, or better.

But merely improving the vesting of pension rights will not solve everything. In a contributory plan with career-average benefits, for example, the young employee may be paying for all of his currently accruing pension rights while the older employee is being heavily subsidized by the employer, since each unit of his pension costs much more. So if we vest pensions earlier, in these cases, and lock up the contributions of the young employee earlier, are we helping him?

Perhaps where employee contributions are thus locked in, a minimum employer subsidy, such as not less than 25%, should be locked in with it and converted to pension. Or there should be some equivalent recognition of the mutuality of a pension plan between employer and employee regardless of the age of the employee. Where the terminating employee transfers his contributions to his own RRSP, this extra amount or some extra amount based on employer contributions, could well go along with it. Where plans are non-contributory, the point mentioned does not arise, but the RRSP could still be used. In fact, the RRSPs may turn out to be the key to real portability of private pensions, avoiding the need for a cumbersome central pension agency which could be the only other solution.

There are other interesting approaches to solving this problem of transferability, such as a more widespread use of industry-wide plans and reciprocity agreements between plans which enable the roving employee to continue to be covered in the same plan, or to move his service credits along with him. As to benefit design, we seem to see the shadow of a more widespread use of a unit credit formula, with a money-purchase minimum benefit—a combination seldom used until now, but perhaps fitting today's needs.

J. Wells Bentley, widely-experienced Superintendent of Pensions in Ontario, suggested recently at a meeting of the Canadian Pension Conference in Ottawa that:

—Vesting requirements should be liberalized particularly for the *older, short-service* employees, whose concern as to the preservation of their accruing pension rights is especially urgent, since

119

their opportunity to replace lost pensions before retirement is closing up with the years.

—Further, that much good could come from the establishment of a "community pension plan" to serve all of those living in a particular area, so that all the small people could enjoy the same protection and advantages of scale as employees of a big corporation.

These are two excellent suggestions. Each is aimed into an area where improvement is needed.

We thus come up with a combination that seems to be able to solve the greatest of all problems in the pension field in Canada today, namely the questions of coverage and portability. This combination would include:

1. Compulsory minimum provision for pensions for all workers, just as we have compulsory minimum wage standards.

2. Minimum employer-matching requirements, regardless of age, where plans are contributory.

3. Greatly improved vesting requirements, particularly as to these minimum amounts, and increasingly (as to any additional pension) for the benefit of older terminating employees.

4. Expansion of the role of RRSPs as a vehicle to facilitate portability and accumulation of fragments of pensions for the benefit of those who change jobs often.

It is for Canadians to evaluate these proposals, and if they are acceptable, to bring about such legislative and regulatory changes as will enable them to be effective. *In combination, they would be far healthier for the nation and its economy than the too-glib alternative of relying on the taxing power of the government, enormously increasing the burden on the next generation, doing nothing to provide the source of the benefits, and adding to inflationary pressures—which is what is implied by an expansion of the CPP.* These suggestions would instead emphasize a healthy independence and a growing and strengthening economy, along with full coverage and portability.

What is suggested here would increase overall pension costs, but the effects of not acting somewhat along these lines could lead in short order to a far more costly and less healthy alternative. If it can be accepted that pension costs will tend to rise anyway, this probably indicates a suitable direction for that increase.

2. Survivor benefits:

While many pension plans make provision in one way or another for the survivors of deceased workers and pensioners, and much protection is provided for these same people through individual and group insurance and through the public plans, yet it is nevertheless true that there is room for real improvements in this area.

Four fifths of men die before their wives, and the expectation of life in widowhood after the death of a male pensioner is about seven years. With these basic facts before us, it is a bit extraordinary how rough and cavalier is so often the attitude at the bargaining table toward the inclusion of survivor pensions in the benefit provisions of a pension plan. Usually the whole emphasis is on larger basic pensions and earlier retirement.

Very often provision is made, however, on an optional basis, with the retiring employee choosing between a higher pension to cease when he dies, or a lower pension with a portion to continue to his surviving spouse. In the great majority of cases he does not choose the lower pension. And if the retiring employee is female, she almost never does.

To some extent we are at a social crossroads here. The rights of the spouse who cares for the home are gaining more and more attention and priority. And the long-neglected position of the widow who, after sharing all the years of toil, is left with nothing more than a private pension abruptly terminated when her husband dies, is not what the system is designed to provide.

Working at cross purposes with the humanitarian view suggested here, we have the phenomenon of the surge of women into the work force, their earning of pension credits and C/QPP benefits in their own right, their rejection of the role of economic dependency, the widespread and vast increase in divorce and "serial monogamy," and in many cases the outright rejection of marriage, or of the permanency of marriage, as a way of life. This trend is world-wide. A recent U.S. census report shows that the number of Americans aged 20-34 who have never married jumped 50% over the last five years, while the median age for first marriage is rising.

Pension plans are intimately and sensitively interwoven with the complex fabric of society and the economy. While changes are certainly occurring in society, especially among the younger people, we cannot simply ignore the position of those who have lived according to the older standards, and who find themselves facing a future in old age with no provision for income other than the OAS and such survivor pension as the CPP provides. While most private plans do include joint-and-survivor options, perhaps something a bit stronger is needed.

When the new pensions legislation was being drafted in the United States this problem was resolved by requiring that the normal form of the pension must be a joint-and-survivor benefit if the plan member had been married during the twelve-month period prior to the commencement date of the pension, with the spouse's annuity to be at least one-half the joint annuity. However, the plan member can elect *not* to have this type of pension. So the onus is on the retiring employee to opt *out*, not to *select* the survivor form of pension. This simple change will no doubt greatly increase the protection of widows covered by U.S. pension plans.

Is this enough? There are some plans that go much further, providing a widow pension as an *added*, not an *optional* benefit. Would that be too much? In our changing society, there would be many difficulties in determining eligibility. And there would be added cost unless the basic pension were set more modestly. In one way or another, the private plans would do well to provide something better for survivors than at present.

3. Aftermath of inflation:

We have had an unprecedented inflation in recent years. Those who retired, often compulsorily, in former years under pension plans providing fixed benefits, have watched the dollar shrink and their grocery bills and local taxes increase unmercifully. The OAS/GIS benefits have increased and been indexed, and so have the C/QPP benefits, though many former employees retired before the C/QPP had time to mature, or before it was established.

For those employers who have not already done so, it is time to look at the situation of these pensioners. Unions have, in many bargaining sessions, agreed to the diversion of a portion of the newly won increase for the updating of existing pensions already in course of payment. We have shown earlier that full and unlimited indexing of private pensions is not called for, but the relief of

122

pensioners who have had to suffer the full impact of all of the "excess" inflation of recent years certainly is called for.

In establishing these private pension plans with their provisions for compulsory retirement, and in distributing booklets illustrating the "golden years" in retirement, employers do create expectations and inducements to remain in service right through to the normal retirement age, and then to retire. There is a mutuality of interest, and a basic understanding and trust are created. The employee is entitled to rely on the working out of the system as it has been presented to him, and having done his part, to expect the employer to make every effort to see that the system accomplishes what was intended.

When inflation erodes the pension to the extent that we have seen in recent years, and the employer takes no step to bring relief to the pensioner who served him well, it is understandable that complaints arise and criticisms are levelled at the system.

Many employers have seen fit to adjust pensions in one way or another in recognition of this situation, and, as mentioned, many unions have agreed or taken the initiative to restore the basic intent of these plans. But information is not easily obtainable as to the extent of these adjustments, and there is no question that much remains to be done.

Again we are suggesting steps that involve cost. But among the alternative ways of improving these plans, there cannot be many which would outrank the restoration of pensions destroyed by forces beyond the control of the pensioner, so that the system will function properly.

It is sometimes said that present stockholders have no obligation to those who are no longer working for a company, and that the payment of the full pension which was promised is a complete discharge of the contract, and that inflation is outside the control of and not the responsibility of the employer. This is a hard and legalistic view, and not very humane. Views such as this are what give rise to pressure for legislated reforms. It would be much better for those employers and unions which have not done so to look into this aspect of their plans, and see that they are working satisfactorily.

Easing the financial pinch

In all of the foregoing suggestions to improve the practical working of pension plans, we have been coming up with ideas that will add cost, and hence create problems and difficulties for employers who have to meet these costs.

There is one thing that can be done to ease this problem greatly, and if employers are to be expected to do their part in making these socially desirable but costly improvements, they are in all fairness entitled to all the help and consideration they can get in doing this.

This one thing is to get rid of the five-year funding requirement relating to "experience deficiencies," which is a capricious, harsh, and burdensome regulation, which has had effects that could never have been intended. It has done too much damage to the private pension movement already. It is time to eliminate it.

Scrapping this requirement would cost nothing at all and would inconvenience nobody, but it would certainly go a long way to enabling employers to deal rationally and sensibly with the funding of their pension plans.

It would remove a problem that is giving conniptions to financial vice-presidents, and driving consulting actuaries to the furthest limits of their ingenuity in seeking ways to get around it, sometimes with the connivance of government officials.

In short, eliminating the five-year rule would remove more inhibitions and distortions from the sensible design of the benefit provisions of pension plans, than anything else.

Soaking the poor

In view of their benign effects in assisting people to live in comfort in their later years, to eliminate welfare costs, and to contribute to the health of the economy, pension plans are accorded a certain measure of freedom from income taxes. Contributions of both employers and employees are deductible, within limits, from income for tax purposes, and the investment earnings of pension funds are exempted from liability to pay income taxes. Or are they?

A pension fund can be looked at as nothing more than the savings of a large number of people, brought together for investment and risk-sharing purposes.

If an individual owns a portion of the shares, that is, the risk capital, of a company which pays income taxes on its earnings, and pays dividends from what is left, then the government, in recognition of these corporate taxes, will reduce the taxes paid by the individual so that he is not double-taxed. This is only fair.

But if a pension fund owns these very same shares, there is no such remission of taxes, and the elderly retired employee pays full income tax on his pension, as well as having indirectly but most effectively paid taxes on the investment earnings of his pension fund. So he is at a disadvantage, and is doubly taxed.

Pension funds are investing more and more in the equity capital of industry. This is very good for the economy which desperately needs this capital to provide jobs and increase productivity and pay pensions and taxes. The continued investment of pension funds in equity shares is to be encouraged. But this tax treatment works in the wrong direction. Interest on bonds is deductible by the corporation. Dividends on shares are not. This difference creates forces in the economy that lean against equity financing, because the yield from it is taxed more heavily than the yield from debt financing. This does not favor the risk taker, the person on whom we all depend to get the wheels of production started.

And it leads straight to the double-taxation of the pensioner, the last person whom we would wish to see subjected to such penalty.

The 1967 Royal Commission on Taxation, in Volume 1 of its report as outlined by CCH Canadian Ltd., laid down this principle: "The Taxation of People Versus the Taxation of Organizations: All taxes are ultimately borne by people through the reduction of their command over goods and services for personal use. Taxes can, of course, be collected not only from people but also from corporations, trusts and co-operatives. But organizations as such cannot bear taxes. It is for the people who work for, sell to, buy from, or are members, beneficiaries or owners of these legal entities who are made better off or worse off by taxes. It is the effect of taxes on the well-being of people that matters."

From this, the Royal Commission went on to propose the system of grossing-up the dividend received by the individual to its pre-tax amount, and then deducting the full amount of the corporate tax paid, limiting its proposal to "resident shareholders." Where the credit exceeded the amount of the tax payable, the taxpayer *would receive a refund.*

Overlooked in these proposals were the pension funds, which are essentially nothing more than *groups* of resident shareholders. It would seem clear enough that if the point had been raised at the time, the same treatment would have been accorded to them. It is not too late to adjust this anomaly by providing the same refunds to pension funds that are now provided to individuals, thus enabling improved pensions to be provided, and avoiding the double taxation of pensioners which now occurs.

There are some who would go even further by eliminating corporate income taxes entirely, thus avoiding the whole complex problem of double taxation, except as to foreign owners. But at least the step shown above should be taken.

Spreading the good word

It is one thing for pension plans to have made a great contribution to well-being in Canada. It is another to see that this contribution keeps on getting better, as we are now proposing. But if there is not sufficient *awareness* of the magnitude and the importance of this role, then ill-conceived, unenlightened policies, founded on misunderstandings and a lack of perception will tend to come into existence and to do great damage.

Because the control of pension plans is diversified and spread among many employers, unions and administrative groups, there is no one megaphone through which they can all speak at once with a single voice. Nor are they all controlled by a dictator or government armed with a giant bull-horn. They belong closer to the people. Perhaps they need a voice, a way of being heard amid the turbulence of politics and the insistent voices of the various pressure groups. The Canadian Pension Conference, with its broad cross-section of interests and wide geographic spread could perhaps most logically provide the nucleus for some such voice.

But apart from getting a broader awareness of the benign and essential role of private pension plans in the economy, there is within the field covered by each plan, within its own group of members, a constant need for information about the provisions of the plan, and the way it will dovetail with government benefits and with individual needs.

There are those employers and plan administrators who have done well in communicating information to each covered employee about the harvest of benefits protecting the worker and the family members. But there are those who have not, or not yet, done enough in this area, and there are perhaps millions of plan members and family members who simply do not know what is being done for them. Information is nowhere near as expensive as benefits to provide, yet it is sometimes even more appreciated.

CHAPTER SEVEN

Storm Clouds Over the Provinces

"From the point of view of elected officials, of course, it is supremely logical to vote for benefits—but not for the taxes to pay for them. In this way, the politicians win support of public employees, but do not alienate taxpayers, because costs won't be felt during their political tenure."

Barbara Patocka, senior editor, Institutional Investor

"If this country is to maintain effective checks and balances in its political system, public officials must be held accountable for the financial affairs of the activities in the government for which they are responsible. To achieve accountability, effective accounting controls and sound financial reporting are essential."

Arthur Andersen & Co., a U.S. firm of public accountants

In earlier pages of this book, we discussed the prospect faced by the provinces of a drying up of sources of financing arising from the CPP, and even questioned whether the continued pumping of employee and employer CPP taxes into provincial bonds is the best way of investing these funds. Quite apart from the poor interest yield being earned, these bonds do not appear to be doing much toward the building of the productive capital base, or increasing the gross national product. These comments may not seem very helpful to the provinces. However, it is best to state the facts as they are.

This prospective closing out of a source of financing is not the only cloud on the provincial horizon. In addition, there is the prospect that interest will soon have to start flowing *from* the provinces back to the CPP, to service all these loans.

But even this is not the darkest cloud. There are other thunderclouds gathering over the provinces and over the federal government, and through these, over all the taxpayers of Canada. These are the awesome thunderclouds threatening us with a further deluge of taxation to make good on non-funded, indexed pension commitments already made to civil servants.

It was in 1970, when annual increases in federal civil service pensions were limited by a 2% ceiling, that the extra employee contributions to pay the cost of these was set at one-half of 1% of pay. When the ceiling was removed in 1973, *retroactive to 1970*, carrying up the liability for past-service as well as future-service pensions to entirely new levels, nothing was done about employee contributions which will remain at ½% until 1977, when they will go to 1%. This pays *only a very small fraction* of the extra cost. The remaining cost will fall squarely on the general taxpayer, who is unaware of what is impending. So far as one can ascertain, this cost has never been measured, estimated, reported or referred to in any public accounts. Yet the enormous commitment is there, and it is growing by leaps and bounds.

The federal pension system, with or without this indexing, is not a funded system. There is an "account" to keep track of the value of "basic" (non-indexed) benefits, but there is not, and never has been, any accumulation of assets to pay for the pensions to be paid in the future to government employees. Complete reliance is placed on the taxing power of the government—which means the taxpayer—to make good on these commitments when the time comes. It would be illegal for a private employer to approach the provision of pensions in this way.

"The gross inequity of the arrangements which now exist as between the public and private sectors of the economy is, however, only part of the story. What is really disturbing is to assess the impact on public policy when the federal civil service has

129

managed to insulate itself from inflation." These are the words of R. M. MacIntosh, executive vice-president of the Bank of Nova Scotia, from an address given on September 25, 1975.

MacIntosh tellingly illustrates his point by quoting a very senior adviser to the Prime Minister who, *after* this pension bonanza had been enacted, observed: "People worry about inflation, but they worry about it in the same way that they worry about rain on their vacation—it really isn't a gut feeling."

This, then, is the kind of determination to stop inflation felt by a highly placed civil servant who has just had his pension indexed without limit.

Pointing out that "the federal pension fund scheme has been set up in almost total disregard for its ultimate cost," MacIntosh further quotes from the Advisory Group on Executive Compensation in the Public Service, the only outside group that examines the federal government's salary and benefits structure: "The cumulative effect of allowing contributions to cease after 35 years, early retirement at the employee's option with 30 years of service at age 55, and of no-limit indexing, *is to produce a situation in which there can be a staggering increase in costs over which management would have little effective control.*"

Such is the situation at the level of the federal government with its 350,000 highly privileged civil servants, all nicely set up with something that the taxpayer, who has to pay for all this, cannot have. What then of the provinces?

There is no difficulty in obtaining information about the *benefit* structure of the pension plans for provincial civil servants. This is public information. Nor is it so difficult to gather statistics as to the number of plan members and pensioners. There is nothing secret or confidential about this. But when one tries to peer into the darker side of these plans, the size of the liabilities that have been building up under them, and how these relate to such assets as exist, there are immediate defenses, difficulties, problems.

These were encountered:

1. No actuarial studies have ever been made; or
2. There is no fund; or
3. The last actuarial study is three years out of date; or
4. The plan is undergoing changes; or
5. The actuary is unable to obtain permission to release any

figures to anyone, not to the Canadian Pension Conference or anyone else.

In some provinces where there is willingness to disclose this type of information, it simply does not exist. In those where recent actuarial studies have been made, their disclosure may be felt to be so hazardous to the credit or the political situation in the province that it would be "unwise" or "extremely dangerous" to let it come out.

In the absence of this information, which one would think the public is absolutely entitled to have, and not wishing to damage the credit rating of any province, we have decided here to discuss the situation in general terms only, without naming any one province, and to talk about the aggregate of all the provinces combined. Even on that basis, the picture is staggering enough.

Following the example of the federal government, most of the provincial governments have provided basic benefits exactly matching or closely similar to the federal government benefits. There are some differences in the early retirement and escalation provisions. In these, most but not all of the provinces are less liberal than the federal government; nearly all are far more liberal than private industry. The funding situation varies widely and is generally very poor indeed. There are cavernous actuarial deficiencies. In these pages we shall comment in some greater detail on the benefit commitments, particularly as to indexing or escalation, the funding and cost aspects of these plans, and the reporting or disclosure to the public whose money is involved. We shall look at the question of how the funding of all these plans in combination would compare with those of New York City when it collapsed, and we shall examine briefly the actuarial and accounting principles that are involved.

Benefit commitments and escalation

All provinces provide generous 2% final-average benefit formulas, integrated with CPP, with a final-average earnings base of three, four, five, six or seven years. Two provinces index these without limit, two use an 8% and one a 6% limit on annual increases, two review pensions at regular intervals, two have provided no information, one is reviewing its escalation policy.

Full (unreduced) pension can begin as early as age 55 in three provinces (with 30, 32 and 35 years service), at age 60 in eight provinces (with 10, 20, 25 or in one case 30 years service). Only five provinces make any reference at all to age 65. Some provinces provide for alternative qualifications—hence the apparent overlap.

Funding practices

These vary widely from total disregard of funding pension obligations, in which employee contributions are simply treated as revenue (three provinces), to non-funding of employer-paid pensions but accumulating employee contributions (two provinces), to matching employee contributions as paid and later making up the deficiency (four provinces), to "payments on an ad hoc basis."

It is a very sick picture, and in no way in keeping with either the liberal approach to benefits and elibigility, or with what these provincial governments require of all private plans within their jurisdiction.

Reporting and disclosure

The principle of determining and reporting the value of benefits as the obligation to provide them accrues, and the unfunded liability for all benefit rights and expectations that have been created, is simply not followed at all.

By making cross-comparisons between the U.S. federal civil service retirement system, which has been the subject of a better class of actuarial analysis, and the Canadian federal and provincial systems, many of which have not, one can manage to discern some of the shadowy outlines of the liabilities which exist unrecognized in Canada.

For example, the introduction of only a 4% allowance for future annual inflation (with allowance for a "kicker") jumped the assessed value of the U.S. federal plan, as a percentage of payroll, by 150%. A similar proportionate increase in Canada (which would correspond, without the "kicker," to an inflation rate of about 5.3% annually) would carry the officially reported mix of *14.2% and 11.4%* (male and female) of payroll (which excludes inflation allowances) all the way up to *32.5% of payroll.* This gives some idea of what is being stored up for future taxpayers. The provision of these benefits depends wholly on the taxing power of the government—and on the taxpayer.

The situation in the provinces differs only in degree. Those which have no fund assets at all, or which have accumulated nothing more than employee contributions, are building liabilities at an alarming rate. Those which are matching employee contributions, and believe that this provides a satisfactory approach to funding, are working under an illusion. Especially where escalation is automatic and unlimited, or capped at a high annual rate, liabilities are growing at rates far in excess of assets. Even where full escalation is not committed in advance, but is nevertheless practiced in stages, the long-term effects will be the same, even though the actual commitment is less.

How does all of this compare with the tragic example of New York City? When all these public plans in Canada are lumped together, and the assets and liabilities (so far as these can be roughly estimated) are brought face to face, and contribution rates and (crudely calculated) benefit costs are matched, one emerges with the unhappy conclusion that *Canada is in worse shape than New York.*

At least New York did make an outward showing of funding its plans. True, the actuarial basis was outdated and moth-eaten in the extreme. But at least some effort was made, and $7 billion in reserve funds were built up, which helped to keep the city going in its time of crisis and collapse.

"Thank you very much, New York," was the comment of one consulting actuary long experienced with state and local-government pension plans. "Thank you for showing that even the taxing power of the government has its limits."

The tax base of New York includes the world headquarters of 385 of the 500 biggest companies in America. Even that did not prove adequate, and huge cutbacks in benefits are now in process of negotiation. The pension plans in New York seem older and more mature than those in Canada. There had been time for the pension rolls to swell to their full size, and benefit outflows were simply enormous. It is all a preview of where Canada seems to be going.

Standards and principles

The Society of Actuaries, which examines the fitness of actuarial students to become professionals in either Canada or in the United States, has two national counterparts, the Canadian Institute of Actuaries, and the American Academy of Actuaries. Of these, the Academy has recently come out with a statement of principles that should be observed in evaluating the liabilities under pension plans, and in dealing with the problem of inflation. These include:

—"The actuary should take into account any material effects of inflation . . . The anticipated effects of inflation . . . should be explicitly recognized . . .

—". . . The actuary has an obligation to disclose his assumptions regarding inflationary effects. If future inflationary conditions are not anticipated on a basis that seems realistic . . . he has a further obligation to indicate approximately what results would be obtained if more realistic inflationary allowances were to be made.

—". . . The actuary should disclose the trend of the funding pattern, and should indicate . . . the impact of such funding pattern on future pension contributions."

The Accounting Principles Board in the United States also has laid down principles dealing with the recognition and disclosure of costs arising under pension plans, and their treatment as a current cost at the time when the obligation accrues. In its analysis of the financial reporting of costs under the U.S. federal government, Arthur Andersen & Co. includes this key paragraph:

"Liabilities for . . . retirement benefits . . . under civil service have been recorded, irrespective of whether trust funds exist for the programs, *because the liabilities are those of the government and not of the trust funds, and since covered individuals worked directly for the government.*"

Though various projections have been made relative to the CPP, one finds in the public accounts no statement of the liabilities which have built up under the OAS/GIS legislation, under the CPP, under the Supplementary Retirement Benefits provisions for civil servants, or under the various provincial plans. All of these rely very heavily, or exclusively, on the taxing power of

134

the government. *The taxpayers are not being informed.*

"The basic appeal of a pay-as-you-go approach, as opposed to a funded system, is that it permits generous commitments to be made with low visibility to the tax payer," stated Tax Foundation, Inc., in its 1976 study, "Employee Pension Systems in State and Local Government."

Fiscal discipline

The study also noted: ". . . .Funding imposes fiscal discipline and responsibility on public authorities . . . Theoretically a government can make no contributions until employees begin to retire. With the first large wave of retirees, however, costs become disproportionately large . . . the money may be extremely difficult to obtain."

At the University of Pennsylvania's Wharton School, Dr. Dan McGill, who is chairman of the Pension Research Council, has a project going to study the actuarial foundations of public plans. He says this:

"One of the strongest arguments [for funding public plans] is that funding imposes discipline on state and local authorities, who have gotten completely out of hand as far as liberality goes. They keep lowering the eligible retirement age without any reduction in pension benefits . . . In many plans, it's down to 55, where in most corporations it's still 65. And there are no legislative restraints on this sort of thing. Public officials see this as a way to curry favor among their employees . . . They can give increased benefits without having to pay for the increase now. The theory is: Let someone else worry about that 40 years from now."

Just as the provincial pension funding scene in Canada is in a state of disarray and deficiency so also in the United States one finds many varied stages and varieties of funding among the state retirement systems. There is, however, this difference:

In the United States, out of 50 states, *only one* (Massachusetts) has no pension fund, and that state is now under such severe financial pressure that all pay increases to active employees had to be deferred for some years. In Canada, out of 10 provinces, *three* have no fund at all, and *two* do no funding of employer-paid benefits.

135

Need for reform

The following further extracts from the 1976 study published by the Tax Foundation in the U.S. should be noted by all Canadians:

"The financial difficulties of some states and municipalities have been attributed, at least in part, to the conspicuous enrichment in pension benefits which public employees have won for themselves . . .

". . . Public-employee retirement benefits have become so generous as to place many private-sector workers in an unfair, disadvantaged position.

"One particularly hard-hitting statement . . . was made by former Representative Martha W. Griffiths of Michigan: 'People must awaken to the tax burden that is being placed on the average taxpayer by these retirement systems. It is totally unfair, in my judgment, to give a public worker a pension after 20 or 30 years of work that is so high that you are, in effect, paying for each job two or three times.'

". . . Many government pension plans need reform more than private plans . . . Problems of financing the private plans may appear minor when compared with those some government units will face."

In the American pension reform legislation enacted in 1974, there is the requirement that four committees be appointed to make studies of government pension systems and report back to Congress. These committees are to probe into such aspects as the vesting and financing or funding of benefits, fiduciary arrangements, and the necessity for federal legislation and standards with respect to public plans, including minimum funding standards, as well as the taxing power of governments in maintaining the plans.

Should we not be thinking along these same lines in Canada? Or is it safe to go on blindly abusing the taxing power of future governments, and the taxpaying ability of future generations of taxpayers, with no enquiry, no measurement, no accounting to the public, no recognition in actuarial studies of inflation's impact on presently accruing liabilities, or disclosure of the results to those whose money is involved?

On the question of disclosure of the facts to the public, the Tax

Foundation in the U.S. has this to say: "In a number of cities which have inadequately financed their retirement plans, municipal administrations have hidden this fact and its attendant consequences from the public by such subterfuges and financial gimmickry as underestimating the costs incurred and simply refusing to disclose the terms of pension agreements entered into."

Reverting to the example of New York, it is reported that financial deterioration resulted from two faulty practices:

1. Use of obsolete actuarial assumptions, dating from the 1908-1914 period, so that pension cost estimates and resulting contributions from the City were understated.

2. Employment of financial "sleight of hand" and fiscal gimmickry to further reduce payment of these understated funding needs.

At the same time, New York City made a practice of not publicizing the terms of its pension contracts, making it difficult or impossible for an outside observer to glean any impression of the true state of affairs.

Nor has there been sufficient emphasis placed on the fact that a soundly funded pension plan is *much cheaper* in the long run than an unfunded or "pay-as-you-go" plan. Not only are there invested reserves which generate enough income over the long period to pay for *about one half* of the pensions paid out; there is also a more even flow of cost, a cushion to fall back on in a time of temporary difficulty in making payments, the avoidance of a build-up of excessive cost after a decade or two, and a far greater assurance to employees that they will actually receive the pensions promised.

It is extraordinary that employee organizations in Canada have not seen fit to exert more pressure to get provincial and similar plans placed on a sounder actuarial basis than at present. The inevitable price of benefit cut-backs is now being faced in many public plans in the United States where faulty funding practices had been followed. In some cases, this is no bad thing, since the benefits themselves had been blown out of proportion. But it is worth recording that, for example, in New York the retirement age for new "general" employees has been raised from 55 to 62 years, and ceilings have been placed on benefits, such as 60% of final salary up to $12,000 and 50% of pay above that.

It is a sobering fact that the plans for public employees in Canada, taken together, provide benefits on a *far more liberal basis* than that, and are *even less soundly funded.*

Take another U.S. example, the city of Hamtramck, Michigan. In the late 1940s the city was told that the funded cost of its police and fire pension plans was 25% of payroll. That looked ridiculous, so it was not paid. By 1955, an actuarial study showed the cost had grown to 50% of payroll. Again, these costs were not met. So, by 1970, Hamtramck was shelling out 70% of payroll just to pay current pensioners. Soon the city ran right out of money, and had to suspend both current salaries of active workers and also pension payments. Many other cities have drifted very close to this same precipice.

One proposal, designed to take the financial sting out of early retirement, would have the employee who leaves service before age 60 wait until age 60 before commencing to draw his pension— a measure that would make a big difference to the cost of police and firemen's pensions, for example, not to mention other civil service pensions.

Drifting into trouble

The list of states and cities drifting into trouble could easily be extended to include Atlanta (threatened with an insolvent system); Philadelphia and Pittsburgh (reserves $800 million short); Lakewood, Ohio (pension payments suspended, legislature and voters unwilling to waive limitations on municipal taxing authority); Detroit (court ruled special property tax had to be paid to satisfy pension costs); Illinois (ordered to pay $1.7 billion liability in teachers' retirement system); Delaware (had to double annual pension contributions to get system on a sound footing); Sacramento (actuarial basis did not recognize inflation though benefits indexed); Mississippi (employee contributions raised and new employees placed in less liberal plan); Boston, Indianapolis and Florida (all in critical shape).

In a survey of 122 police pension plans completed by the author in 1971, it was found that 56 were completely non-funded, even though in nearly all cases the police officers themselves had made contributions.

But perhaps Canada can learn the most from Britain, where a besieged economy is faced with the need to automatically increase pensions to a million retired civil servants. "If it does pay the increases, it will enrage the people whose taxes will be raised or futures mortgaged . . . whose pay has been sharply limited by . . . government wage policy, and all private pensioners who are guaranteed no increases," reports the Globe and Mail on July 8, 1976. It is also reported that Sir Geoffrey Howe has estimated that "to buy fully inflation-proof pensions for a million civil servants at current market rates would cost £355 billion—three times the total wealth of the United Kingdom."

Turning to Canada, this article states: "Canada can look forward to some unhappy parallels with the British situation . . . A group of Canadians have been set aside to receive a benefit not assured to the rest of Canadians . . . Canadians are fighting inflation. Yet a privileged group in their midst is not required to join the battle, ever. The costs could eventually be as grave for the economy as Britain now finds them . . . The situation is unfair . . ."

An explanation that backfired

On October 18, 1976, the Treasury Board in Ottawa released a statement entitled "Basic Facts about Pensions in the Public Service in Canada." Undoubtedly prepared by civil servants whose own pensions were involved, this masterpiece of half-revelation, which was given very wide circulation by the Treasury Board, set out to show that:

(a) The Public Service Pension Plan is financially sound;

(b) Its total costs have not been out of line;

(c) Employee contribution rates are above average;

(d) Its early retirement provisions are "comparable to those of numerous private plans";

(e) Liabilities from indexing benefits are unlikely to increase its costs as a proportion of payroll.

Stated the Treasury Board:

"Basic pensions . . . are financed in accordance with the same actuarial principles as those which generally apply to private sector plans."

"Recent statements claiming or implying that the whole program is financed on a pay-as-you-go basis are therefore off the mark."

"Much of the recent discussion . . . has overlooked or ignored . . . that public servants make above-average contributions . . .

"Another . . . misunderstanding . . . arises from speculation . . . about the size of the pensions being received by a few recently retired senior public servants. This has created an impression that Public Service pensioners typically receive pensions greatly exceeding those of most working Canadians."

"Recent allegations that public servants live in a 'pension paradise' and receive 'fat' and 'limitless' pensions are . . . devoid of factual basis."

In this vein, and supported by numerous tables of figures, the statement seeks to establish both the reasonableness of benefit levels and the soundness of funding procedures used by the federal government in Ottawa with respect to its employees.

It is one thing for a situation of unfair and unjustifiable privilege to exist at the expense of taxpayers. It is another for a responsible and highly placed government department, steeped in conflict of interest, to issue material of this kind, carefully showing one aspect of the situation, and in so doing to make statements about actuarial soundness, benefit comparisons and similar technical matters, that simply do not stand up to examination. This does nothing to advance the credibility of the government.

Outraged by what had been done, the Council of the Canadian Institute of Actuaries promptly responded in November 1976 with these broadsides:

"This document, which was tabled in the House of Commons on October 18, 1976, by the President of the Treasury Board, purports to defend the Public Service pension system against criticisms which have been leveled against it. What is ironic is that the speciousness or the dubious validity of so many of the statements made and arguments advanced in this document have aroused the suspicion or outright condemnation of practically every professional actuary who has examined the document. The Institute does not propose in this statement to rebut in detail all of these dubious statements and arguments, although we are quite prepared to do so if that becomes necessary. We believe it is more constructive to address ourselves to two key questions.

140

"1. Is the system being properly financed?

"2. How do the benefits provided by the system compare with those of other Canadian employers?"

While not criticizing the funding of the "basic" pensions, the Council had this to say about the portion of the benefits arising from the indexing mechanism:

"In determining the contributions under this part of the system, no attempt is made to recognize the currently accruing cost, nor is there any requirement that the actual experience be subject to periodic actuarial review, as is the case for the basic part of the system. The result, in our opinion, is that *the value or cost of the indexing adjustments is systematically concealed and deferred for payment by future generations of taxpayers and public servants.*"

Turning to the benefit levels, the Council stated:

"Here we are dealing with facts which are familiar to most practitioners in the pension field . . . *The benefits provided by the Public Service system, taken as a whole, are more generous (and in most cases much more generous) than those provided by the plans of practically all private-sector employers* . . . Public Service employees contribute to their plan at a higher rate than most employees . . . but they are more than compensated . . . by the generous . . . benefits. Given a thorough . . . understanding of these benefits . . . most private sector employees would be only too happy to contribute at a comparable rate if their employers would agree to provide comparable benefits."

The Council concludes that these generous benefits combined with "inadequate current recognition of costs" are a cause of concern, that when the indexed extra benefits are recognized and costed actuarially "it will be possible to begin a more rational consideration of the design of the benefits," providing the public with a much clearer picture of the true costs of the Public Service system, which is presently "so deficient."

The Council of the Canadian Institute of Actuaries is not alone. Other well-qualified critics have expressed a chorus of displeasure at the approach of the Treasury Board, pointing out that the *value* of employer-provided public service pensions is *more than twice* that of private pensions, that the so-called fund assets are nothing more than a bookkeeping entry on paper, and that future taxpayers have indeed a reason for grave concern.

It would indeed be a constructive step for the federal government to set an example both by cutting back its overgenerous pension provisions before they cause further problems, and by setting up real reserves on a sound basis which can contribute in a real way to the strengthening of the Canadian economy.

To his great credit, Martin O'Connell has recently suggested (in a speech to the Canadian Pension Conference in Montreal, December 7, 1976) that the present highly liberal pension arrangements applying to Members of Parliament be also cut back.

As one moves from the federal and provincial plans in Canada to the level of the Crown corporations and similar organizations, a more satisfactory level of funding and fiscal responsibility seems generally to be shown, and the provisions of the various legislated funding standards seem to be more closely observed or approached. But even here caution is needed, since the benefit practices of the senior plans with their open-ended indexing are often carried into these semi-government plans. Unless stiff actuarial assumptions, adhering to the standards outlined above, are used, there can be the appearance but not the substance of sound funding.

In an earlier page we threw out the hint that Canada may be sitting on unfunded liabilities under its public pension systems of some $400 billion. That was not a blind guess. If the federal civil service and all these provincial and local systems are thrown in, it may be low.

CHAPTER EIGHT

Transition

"Civil servants should always bear in mind the distinction between being permitted to retire compulsorily and compelled to retire voluntarily."

A British civil servant

Beneath the outer showing of fine distinctions, technicalities, complexities and niceties of design and presentation, and the apparent permanence of pension plans, there are vast if gradual changes and deep inner forces at work. The origins of some of these are demographic. The roots of others lie in technological evolution, in the rise of computers and synthetics and mass production, and the changing proportions of the work force as the emphasis moves from primary to secondary, to tertiary, and to post-industrial occupations.

Changing social values and concepts of marriage, as birth rates fall and women leave the home and enter the paid work force, the long rise in material living standards, and growing expectations of leisure all play their part in this complex dance of interweaving social and economic values. But like dark shadows on the stage of western civilization, there loom the threats of future population pressures from abroad, food and raw material scarcities and famines, pollution, and urban crises, mocking all our values and expectations, and calling into question the whole basis of civilization itself.

While these forces and changes are working themselves out, pension planners, trying to discern what the world will be like a generation or two hence, are not finding it easy to sense what exactly we should be aiming to accomplish as between:

—Replacing the *whole* income or purchasing power of a person leaving the work force after a reasonable period of work, or

—Providing a *sufficient* income to meet essential needs, with something additional for reasonable comfort, or

—Providing a *second* income commencing at an age or after a period of service considered reasonable, so that the person can continue to work indefinitely but enjoy two incomes, and possibly even more later.

Nor is it easy to see whether:

—Rising productivity can be counted on to enable people to work less years, so that retirement should take place *sooner*, or

—The ultimate demographic burden of pensioners, combined with a shrunken population of workers, will cause today's concepts of the retirement age to become outdated, leading to *later* retirement, or

—Lengthening expectations of life at all ages should logically lead to a *longer* work life, or

—The shrinkage in work-life due to rising productivity should be *distributed* throughout life, via longer vacations and sabbatical leaves, and not all saved up and concentrated in a more prolonged retirement, or

—If we wish to maintain our material standards as world population doubles and more, and resources continue to be depleted, we may not be able to cope with a great and continuing relative expansion of retired people living in leisure and making no contribution to the economy, indicating a *later* retirement age in the long term, or

—Since the surge of young people and women into the work force is causing overcrowding and unemployment in the short term, this can be relieved to some extent by *accelerating* retirement now, or

—Since people do not all age at the same speed, each person is

144

unique, and individual needs and situations are all different, it would therefore follow that there should be *no fixed retirement age* at all.

Some of these arguments flow from the long term, some from the short term viewpoint; some from the viewpoint of society or the economy as a whole, some from the individual position. For those who have survived the conditions of full war mobilization, the memories of retired people flocking back into civilian work will serve as a vivid reminder that conditions do not always remain the same, and that changes in social conditions do not always happen at glacial speed.

But, overshadowing all this, there looms another unanswered question.

Utopia: The best is yet to be?

In all our pension planning, in all our booklets describing the golden years, the sunset years, the new freedom from work and want, the release from toil and from the tyranny of the alarm clock, the years of togetherness and fulfillment, we take it all for granted that this life in retirement is just what the worker always wanted. Nor are the professionals and technicians who write these booklets and work in the pension field alone in this.

"No longer do you have to care about worldly achievement; the crucial, life-sustaining necessities are of prime importance—the luxuries and frivolities you dreamed of earlier no longer are. You are at last free to be yourself, unconcerned about status or the opinions of others, unworried about the future. No more are you at the mercy of the tyranny of glands and hormones—or of despotic parents, teachers, employers. Your age group is the only one that can get away with the beachcomber's attitude. Be a beachcomber—at the edge of eternity."

So writes Leopold Bellack, MD, from his experience in psychology and clinical psychiatry, in his book, *The Best Years of Your Life*. And so we have mesmerized a whole generation of workers into thinking that retirement is a time of golden fulfillment, of freedom to travel, of pleasant gratification of earlier dreams, of leisure and that pleasant hedonism that was enjoyed in another golden age by those lotus eaters upon whom the ever-resourceful Odysseus once stumbled in the course of his wanderings. And so, yearning ever for that release from drudgery, for those sweet, golden, sunset years, we buckle down and go about our work.

We have even begun to develop a new status symbol—the escape from full-time work. Whoever has extricated himself from a full-time job has got it made. Not only is he able thus to enjoy the fulfillment of all his dreams; but also between his company pension, his wife's income and his own government (CPP and OAS) benefits, his family income is probably higher than that of many full-time workers. What a position to be in. Real success!

All you have to do to make it is to keep on working until your retirement age. Or does all of this make sense?

Among Canada's more eminent scholars and medical researchers is Dr. Hans Selye, director of the Institute of Experimental Medicine and Surgery at the University of Montreal, a world authority on the body's physiological response to stress, and a Companion of the Order of Canada, this country's highest honor. Based on his 40 years of research into the causes of every kind of stress in people, Dr. Selye has some trenchant things to say about retirement. For example:

"The average citizen would suffer just as much from the boredom of purposeless subsistence as from the inevitable fatigue created from the constant compulsive pursuit of perfection . . . The majority equally dislike a lack of stress and an excess of it . . . the distress of having nothing worthwhile to do or being constantly overtaxed by excessive activity."

Referring to the "gradual displacement of a sense of purpose by a sense of despair" and the "boredom of assured monotony" that are so often the rancid fruits of retirement, Dr. Selye lays it on the line:

—"Man must work . . . We have to begin by clearly realizing that work is a biological necessity. Just as our muscles become flabby and degenerate if not used, so our brain slips into chaos and confusion unless we constantly use it for some work that seems worthwhile to us.

—"For many older people, the most difficult aspect of retirement to bear is the feeling of being useless . . . The continuous leisure of enforced retirement is certainly not an attractive way of

146

life . . . Nothing to do is not rest; a vacant mind and a slothful body suffer the distress of deprivation . . . The fatal enemy of all utopias is boredom.

—"Few things are as frustrating as complete inactivity, the absence of any stimulus, any challenge.

—". . . Frustrations . . . and aimlessness are among the most damaging stressors, and psychosomatic studies have shown how often they cause . . . heart attacks, hypertension, mental disease, suicide, or just hopeless unhappiness.

—"To keep fit, we must exercise both our bodies and our minds.

—"Diversion from one activity to another is more relaxing than complete rest."

It is this last observation that seems to hold the key to a better approach to retirement than the one we have been following. That and Benjamin Franklin's famous aphorism: "There is nothing wrong with retirement as long as one doesn't allow it to interfere with one's work." In expressing these thoughts and observations, Dr. Selye is by no means alone. He is merely the most eminent and most eloquent. These are views we have heard before, and have arrogantly overridden with our juggernaut of compulsory retirement.

The greatest of all strategic errors?

Are we then approaching the whole subject of pensions and retirement from the wrong angle? Are we committing vast funds in this generation, and placing a galling economic yoke upon the necks of the next generation, so that we can achieve a state of utopian slothfulness, unhealthy and dangerous alike to our bodies, our minds and our spirits—so that we can become flabby and degenerate and parasitic and frustrated with aimless boredom? Is this what this great pension movement of our times is all about? Is there no better way?

Perhaps our whole effort, our whole direction, has been wrong. Perhaps we could solve many problems at the same time if we approached the questions of retirement and pensions and the placing of unacceptable burdens on the next generation along new lines. Perhaps we must realize that these new lines would require social changes on a scale that would be compared with the surge of women into the work force, or the establishment and development of our present system of pensions, or social welfare. We have successfully accomplished all three of these at the same time, substantially in the past two or three decades. So what can now be suggested should require no great effort of adjustment; we still have two or three decades to accomplish it before the real heat will arise under our present system.

The history of the world (with one difference)

We will pick up the story in 1939. That was the year when nylon stockings first appeared, and people were dancing the Lambeth Walk. Howard Hughes had just flown around the world. The film Pygmalion starring Leslie Howard had been released. Albert Einstein and Leopold Infeld had published *The Evolution of Physics;* Franz Boas, *General Anthropology;* and Lancelot Hogben, *Science for the Citizen.* Vitamin E had just recently been identified.

Across the Atlantic, things were disturbing. Hitler had appointed himself as War Minister; the Munich conference had taken place the previous September and on October 10, 1938, Germany had occupied the Sudetenland. In Britain, Eden had resigned, and Duff Cooper, First Lord of the Admiralty, had also resigned. So had Czech President Benes, and a puppet president had been appointed. War clouds gathered. Now Germany occupied Bohemia and Moravia, renounced its nonaggression pact with Poland and its naval agreement with Britain, and concluded a 10-year alliance with Italy and a nonaggression pact with Russia. Britain and Poland signed a treaty of mutual assistance. On September 1, Germany invaded Poland, and World War II broke out. Just two months later, King George VI summoned Winston Churchill to Buckingham Palace, and after receiving him graciously, said:

"Winston Spencer Churchill, you have served your country well these long years. I was particularly impressed by your spirited leadership of the outcry against Neville Chamberlain's policies at Munich last year. There is much trouble in the world. Britain is at war, and it would please me very much to think of you back at the

Admiralty, or even holding higher responsibilities.

"But the purpose of this visit is different. As you know, we have a fixed mandatory retirement age of 65, and since you will reach that age this month, the Queen and I would like to present you with some gifts that we hope will help you to fill the pleasant hours in all the days of retirement that now lie before you. We understand that you enjoy landscape painting, so we have decided to present you with this easel, this palette and these brushes and paints. And, oh yes, here is your first pension cheque. May all your golden years be filled with happiness."

And so World War II was lost, freedom and democracy went under, and the history of mankind has never been the same since. *Is this how we would do it today?*

Fortunately for all of us, Winston Churchill did come to full power a few months *after* he reached the "normal retirement age" of 65, and from then on, for many years, gave the world a brilliant example of what a man can achieve when he is supposed, by our present standards, to be finished. While this example is quite arresting and fascinating, it is far from unique. Consider for example the differences in the shaping of world history, and in the richness of human culture, if everything described below, which was done after age 65, had been eliminated.

Let us begin with the golden age Greece, of which it has been said: "All that chains the desire of mankind with a yearning that is never stilled, to that one golden moment in the past whose fair and balanced interplay of perfect flesh and soul no later gains of thought can compensate centres about that bright and stately city of romance [Athens], the home of Pericles and all the Arts, whence from generation to generation has streamed upon ages less illustrious an influence at once the sanest and the most inspired of all that have shaped the secular history of the world."

It was from this era that we have inherited the concepts of freedom and democracy, and it was under the immensely strong, inspiring and understanding leadership of Pericles that this civilization reached its zenith. Many are the famous names and contributions to literature, art, philosophy and science that trace back to the period of his leadership. "The Athenians," he said, "are lovers of beauty without having lost their taste for simplicity, and lovers of wisdom without loss of manly vigor. We are a free democracy, but we obey the laws, more especially those which protect the oppressed, and the unwritten laws whose transgression brings shame."

Greatest of all his orations, in which he enshrined not only for his own people but for countless generations yet unborn his concepts of democracy, Pericles' Funeral Oration stands out even today as the clearest and most comprehensive statement of the ideals of a democratic society that has ever guided the thoughts and actions of mankind. When he delivered this famous oration, Pericles was 69 years old—four years beyond his normal retirement date, though still at the height of his power. The Greek civilization in its full bloom had much to teach the world, but no one had dreamed up the idea of pension plans with mandatory retirement at age 65. That is just as well for all of us.

Charlemagne, the first Holy Roman Emperor, reached his normal retirement age in the year 807, but no one mentioned this to him, and he continued to rule over the vast empire he had conquered for six more years. He did not crown his son Louis the Pious as his successor until 813, when he was 71 years old.

Had Queen Victoria retired at age 65, Britain could never have bathed in the glory of her Golden Jubilee in 1887, and would have missed out on her Diamond Jubilee by 13 years.

Harry Truman reached his normal retirement age in 1949. Did he retire? Not at all. That was the year he was inaugurated President of the United States. The following year he gave instructions to the Atomic Energy Commission to develop the hydrogen bomb, and took the decision to respond to the North Korean invasion of South Korea. That was the start of the Korean War. And in 1951, a full two years after his normal retirement date, he was still spunky enough to fire General Douglas MacArthur.

General Eisenhower was still below age 65 when he was first elected President of the United States, but in 1956, when he should, according to our present concepts, have already spent a year relaxing in a hammock or playing golf, he was re-elected for a second term, and was 67 when he came up with the "Eisenhower Doctrine."

If Marshal Tito had followed our rules, he would have turned over his presidency of Yugoslavia after only four years in the saddle, and some younger "more vigorous" man would have taken his place *19 years ago.*

Charles De Gaulle was another person obviously not covered by one of our modern pension plans. It was not until he was four years beyond our mandatory retirement age that he became President of France, and it was four years after that, at age 73, that he first kept Britain out of the European Common Market.

Genghis Kahn did get in under the wire. His conquest of Persia was at age 63, but he held his empire together as no other man could have done for nine more years, and when he died it was divided into three large empires. No one had handed him his first pension cheque "dated as of January 1 coinciding with or next following his 65th birthday" as we say in our pension plans today. That would have shortened his reign by seven years.

It was also a year before Queen Elizabeth I's normal retirement date that the hostile Spanish Armada came sailing up the channel, so there was no problem on that account. But she had overstayed her normal retirement date by a full three years when she delivered her "Golden Speech" to Parliament, reviewing the achievements of her long and glorious reign, which did not end there.

One could go on to mention such names as Mao Tse-tung, Franco, Adenauer, Haile Selassie, Khruschev, Chiang Kai-shek and many others, none of whom retired at age 65. But enough of these rulers, presidents and conquerors. How about the artists, musicians, scientists, mathematicians, philosophers, writers and all that gentler but no less mighty breed? Were they all washed up at age 65? Well, not exactly. For example:

Michelangelo reached his normal retirement age in the year 1540. But there was no pension plan for him, and instead of sunning himself in Sorrento, he became very busy replanning the Capitol in Rome. A full six years after he should have retired, he designed the famous dome and undertook to complete the construction of St. Peter's in Rome, and when he was *80 years old* in Florence he executed the Pieta, which some would say is the most exquisite piece of sculpture ever done by man. Fifteen years after his normal retirement date!

Goya, although qualified for our OAS, C/QPP and other benefits went right on painting, and the following year did the famous

Duke of Wellington portrait, and four years later, at age 70, the Duke of Osuna.

Matisse, not to be outdone, painted his lovely Young English Girl when he was 78 years old.

Titian was another great and prolific painter. Among his masterpieces, Pope Paul III and Nephews was done when he was 69; Charles V on Horseback at 71; Lavinia at 73; and Venus and Adonis at 77.

Verdi completed his opera Otello when he was 74; and Falstaff at 80.

Voltaire reached age 65 in 1759, and the same year brought out *Candide*, following this up four years later with his *Treatise on Tolerance*, then the *Philosophical Dictionary* a year later, and *Irene* when he was 84.

The great German philosophers Leibniz and Kant each went right on working well after age 65, as did Franz Liszt, Ibsen and many others. Engrossed in their work, they saw no reason to stop at age 65.

Neither John D. Rockefeller nor Charles Schwab, builders of vast industrial empires in more modern times, saw any reason to quit at age 65; nor did famous Supreme Court Justices Oliver Wendell Holmes and William O. Douglas in the United States, or Ivan Rand in Canada.

Einstein, perhaps the greatest physicist who ever lived, and one of those in the team that developed the atom bomb, reached his normal retirement age in 1944, the year before the bomb was dropped on Hiroshima and Nagasaki, bringing World War II to an end. But Einstein did not vegetate. At the age of 71, he published *General Field Theory* (an attempt to expand his famous Theory of Relativity).

Socrates, famed for his wisdom, was still raising fundamental questions about everything long after he was 65, and in fact Plato thought enough of his statements on the last day of his life, when he quaffed the hemlock at age 71, to record them for posterity in his *Apology*.

Goethe, the greatest of all German writers, reached his normal retirement age in 1814, but, undaunted, went on producing masterpieces until his death *18 years later*, at the age of 83, when Part II of *Faust* was published.

Disraeli, one of Britain's greatest author-statesmen, did not become Prime Minister until he was 70, but the following year negotiated the purchase of the famous block of Suez Canal shares from the Khedive of Egypt that paved the way for Queen Victoria to be proclaimed Empress of India when he, Disraeli, was 73, eight years beyond his normal retirement date.

If Buddha and Confucius had decided to quit at age 65, mankind would have been the poorer by a total of eleven years of their benificent work and teachings.

And so the parade goes on. Samuel Johnson, Handel, Galileo, Copernicus, Defoe, Toscanini, Edison, Agatha Christie and Picasso were all active and producing long after reaching age 65. Archimedes was doing geometry on a sandy beach at the age of 75 when he was killed by a rampaging soldier.

Not only is this list of post-65 achievement impressive in itself. It is especially impressive because in much of the period covered, the expectation of life was far shorter than it is today. The average life-span was only 22 years at the beginning of the Christian era, 33 years in the year 1200, 41 years in 1850 and 49 years in 1900, as compared with 71 years now. Not very many people ever survived to age 65 in earlier times. So when we consider all of this accomplishment against that background, can there be any doubt that by encouraging a cessation of work at a fixed age, such as 65, we are throwing away and destroying a priceless asset?

And when we talk of lowering the retirement age to 60 or 55 in *these* days of expanding high-age populations, do we realize what we are sacrificing?

Who started this whole idea of retirement at age 65? It was Prince Bismarck, in Germany, when the average expectation of life was only about 45 years, so there was much less involved than there is today. So what did Prince Bismarck himself do? He reached his normal retirement age in 1880. Did he retire? Not at all. He was three years *past* his retirement age when, as Chancellor of Prussia, he introduced a social insurance system of sorts in Germany and he went on governing the country until he was fully 10 years past the retirement age that he himself had laid down.

Example is better than precept.

Two great illusions

In our national approach to pensions (and our tendency to drift toward unfunded, indexed pensions starting earlier) we seem to be operating on the basis of these two fundamentals:

1. That work is evil and is to be avoided if possible; that there is something desirable about *not* working productively after some point in age; or that we are not *capable* of working efficiently after that age, and therefore need help; or that we are not *needed* and may in fact be a nuisance and an impediment to our organization after that age and should therefore be eased out. But regardless of the reason, we should be on our way out of the work force and placed in a position to live by being provided with a pension in return for which we do nothing. What we do with our time after that is in no way important.

2. With the whole nation oriented along these lines, there will always be ample money available to provide these pensions simply by taxing everybody enough to raise whatever is needed. Furthermore, these pensions should be paid to everybody who has reached the retirement age whether they are needed or not, and whether the recipient has retired or not, and the pensions should be continuous and protected from inflation regardless of the state of the economy or whether all of those who have *not* reached the retirement age are working or not, or even exist in sufficient numbers. Nothing, or almost nothing, need be set aside now to assist in this.

What we have brought out in the earlier parts of this review would seem to call each of these positions sharply into question.

As to the first, we have tried to show, and the determined migration of women into the paid work force should have demonstrated clearly enough, that *work is not as unpleasant as has been assumed in our approach to pension planning*. At least it is better than sitting at home. Why, then, be in such a hurry to quit? While the extra money from paid work is a big consideration, women have provided us with many other strong reasons for preferring productive work to idleness, frustration, and dependency. In cases where the work is dangerous or unpleasant, does the solution not lie rather in *improving the conditions of work* than in the escape through pensions, or in rotating this type of work so that one transfers after a time to less onerous work? Does not a nation happily and productively at work have a better chance of survival in an uncertain world than a nation burdened with excessive idleness?

As to the second position, it is the whole thrust of this report that *the level of taxes needed to provide pensions on the scale envisaged by some of our present would-be reformers simply cannot be expected to be forthcoming.* The demographic realities alone would prevent this if the patience of taxpayers did not run out first. It would be a dangerous illusion to suppose that this nation could long survive the stresses that would be created by implementing a plan to provide non-funded pensions on a large scale to all. And even if such stupendous revenues were raised, would this be the best way of using them? Would it not instead turn out to be counter-productive?

In the long run, it seems to the author that the realities that exist in these two areas must combine to create:

1. A *reversal* of the trend to earlier retirements; a positive emphasis and a social acceptance of the opposite, namely the continuation of a productive life until well after the age accepted today as the normal retirement age, and a rebuilding of social norms around this concept.

2. A recognition of the limits of taxation beyond which it is not wise to attempt to press the electorate.

3. An awareness of the dangers being created through demographic shifts both at home and abroad, before too many precedents are built into our society which would be unsustainable in the longer run.

4. The development, instead, of a more modern approach to work and retirement which would:

—Concentrate on *improving and humanizing the conditions of work itself,* restoring the sense of creativity where this has been destroyed by automation, and eliminating the toll and drag on people inherent in commuting long distances between home and work.

—*Redistribute* the balance between work and leisure through a *longer productive life* with any affordable increase in leisure scattered through it rather than concentrated at the end.

—*Phase out* the active work period *gradually,* replacing the

155

more onerous forms of work by less demanding forms of work, such as part-time or light work, spread over a period of five or even 10 years.

—Recognize the *wide variety* of individual differences that exist among people, such as between their health, vigor, aspirations, family situations and capabilities, and accommodate these differences wherever possible through human and very flexible approaches.

—Design our provisions for pensions and fringe benefits around these principles, avoiding waste, duplications and overlaps, but doing an adequate job of replacing income where this is indeed desirable.

—Avoid "estate building" or "second income" forms of pensions *except where real assets are being created* currently to provide these when they are due; in other words, avoid simply imposing claims on the next generation through taxes yet to be raised, for *luxury forms of pensions* due to commence long before the potential productive life is ended, or which it would be difficult for other reasons to justify.

—Recognize that the pension system is *interwoven* not only in a sociological sense with the work system, so that work and retirement or relief from work are inseparably intertwined, but also that the savings for retirement, the contributions to pension funds, are equally interwoven with the capitalization and productivity of work itself, and hence the ability to provide both pensions and work.

What we need above all in the pension field now is a perception of things to come and a *sense of direction*. There will be change. Changes have been occurring faster in the employment and pension field during the last 10 years than at any previous time. If we are not careful, we will make huge mistakes.

We need, too, to have a *sense of timing*. The surge of population entering the work force now is creating pressure to eliminate workers at the higher ages. This tends to make earlier retirements seem sensible now. In no more than 10 years, this will be reversed. There will be a shrunken generation of new entrants and less pressure or some reversal of pressure for early retirements. Still later, there will be a huge pension-cost surge, a serious unbalance in the pensioner/worker ratio, and an outcry against the burden of all these pensioners. We need to be able to sense the timing in all of this, and to avoid making commitments at this time, in response to conditions that are passing, only to find it most difficult if not impossible later to extricate ourselves from policies in conflict with the times.

To keep pension costs under control, we must keep work itself interesting. We are not just playing a game of numbers. We are talking about the lives of many people, their aspirations and capabilities, and their needs to work and create, to live fully and express themselves, as well as to pay their grocery bills.

Things money cannot buy

". . . It is a matter of common sense that people will take pride and pleasure in their work if they are allowed to participate in shaping the decisions that affect it." That was Jack Jones, MBE, British labor leader.

Also in Britain, in her address delivered before the Royal Society of Arts in London on March 10, 1976, Lynda King Taylor, an adviser to the Work Research Unit of the Department of Employment, pronounced some home truths about productivity, motivation, growth and social justice. These come right in on our target area:

". . . In the repeated attempts to achieve growth, to build a bigger national cake, the most vital ingredient, people—and their motivation—is continually ignored. Emphasis on growth alone can—and does—create an alienated society . . .[which] depicts itself in . . . suicide, divorce, drug addiction, alcoholism . . . tension and dissatisfaction, crime . . . innumerable stresses . . . and through shifts in reasoning, morals, ethics, behavior, until the lines between cause and effect become blurred . . . Little emphasis is placed on gaining *'psychological' income from work*, yet *psychological impoverishment breeds many of the ills* . . . for example: stress and irritability, bloody-mindedness, apathy, carelessness, bad timekeeping, militancy, absenteeism." (Italic emphasis added.)

Is this not a description of what is driving many industrial workers to bargain for earlier rather than later retirement, bigger pensions and more security, so that they can get away, escape from dehumanized work in organizations grown monolithic, auto-

157

mated, and psychologically impoverishing? Taylor: "It has been proven many times that the major disrupters of industrial peace stem from psychological symptoms . . ."

Moving to the things industry can do to meet these needs, Taylor states categorically: "People have very definite psychological needs, and demand their satisfaction . . . People need: security and social order; affection and love; status and success; dignity and self respect; opportunities to learn, achieve, advance; consideration as responsible, democratic people; challenge. Without the opportunity to satisfy these needs, there will be alienation . . . In industry, this erupts between those who manage and are managed.

"The way ahead is to build into people's work lives the opportunity for motivation . . . that employees can and will want to contribute much more than at present . . . The problems of boredom, constraint . . . lack of say . . . are not peculiar to the assembly line . . . What workers are suffering from is not capitalism, but laws and customs concentrating power in the hands of a few . . . I do honestly believe that the problem is . . . one of possessing rights to participate in decisions affecting the day-to-day running of one's work efforts."

From a 1975 opinion research survey, Taylor shows that this need for self-realization concentrates itself mainly in participation in decisions close to the actual job of the worker, though there is also a strong need for personal (not mechanical) communication from management as to all matters affecting the organization. "The grass roots manager can be the prime purveyor or destroyer of job interest and participation . . . It is very difficult to fault a desire to be treated as adults and told more of what is going on," she says, adding: ". . . There are three basic inborn needs—*security, stimulation,* and *identity.* The commonly experienced opposites are *anxiety, boredom* and *anonymity.*"

In all of our efforts in the pension field, we may have done well enough in the matter of security/anxiety, but very poorly with stimulation/boredom, and not at all well with identity/anonymity. We may have to think in a new dimension: More employee participation, *vs.* more pension (among other) costs. Having failed before retirement, by providing insufficient job interest, we create conditions that accelerate retirements, only to fail again by providing the alternative of a life of aimless boredom—unless the employee takes his pension and again seeks work. This is not what the pension movement is all about.

Is this not the key difference between the extraordinary achievements of those great men paraded earlier through these pages, who, without pensions, achieved wonders throughout their later years, and our modern-day generation of office and industrial workers? Without exception, those famous performers found great expression and fulfillment in what they were doing. They scarcely needed pensions. In our automated society, many are faced with boredom and frustration in their work, and are driven to seek relief in retirement, only to lose their souls, in too many cases, in aimless atrophy.

Is not the key to a successful pension system—a system that will not cripple future generations with its cost—the same key that will open wider the gates of productivity? Does it not lie in the involvement and motivation of workers in their jobs, the provision of identity and dignity and two-way communication and responsibility and real satisfaction and enthusiasm and participation in decisions? This has nothing to do with wage levels. It cannot be bought for any price. It has to be grown and learned and developed.

When this has been accomplished, we will be a long way forward in developing a more happily work-oriented and less pension-oriented society, and the pressures for earlier retirement should ease, and the demographic thundercloud that hangs over us now may recede before the advancing tide of workers less motivated to retire.

When looked at in human and economic terms this shift in values is greatly needed now. When looked at in terms of pension costs over future decades, it could be basic to our very survival.

The real needs of pensioners

People leaving or being ejected from the full-time paid work force, and entering their new lives under today's conditions as pensioners, are far more diverse and individual in their approach to their new situation than are the younger generation about to enter the work force. And with all of this variety at retirement, there come many more changes with the years. We who provide these pensions, with all their uniformly printed booklets and administrative forms, their automated cheque-printing and streamlined impersonal administrative systems, would do well to spend more time in research in the field of aging, and in studying what it is that pensioners need *other than* their pension cheque.

For example, there is the problem of creative, interesting self-fulfilling *work*, of being *needed*, of being able to "take something home at the end of a useful day" or to look back with satisfaction at a real service performed. In our retirement counselling, we tend to guide the worker into the world of hobbies, recreation, social groups, retirement homes, health services, government benefits, budgets and indeed everything except a new and challenging second career. We assume that society wants the worker out of the work force, that the worker wants to become—and we help the worker to become—as Dr. Bellak so ably put it, a "beachcomber"; or a "grey-haired hippie," as another (retired) person expressed it.

We do not treat retirement as a *change* of work, but as an *end* of work. Worthwhile social work seems to be the only exception to this. Other than jobs as guards, commissionaires and security men, often filled by retired policemen, there are few if any recognized classes of work normally reserved for those aged above 65. In recent years we have watched open-mouthed as women have invaded the truck-driver's cab, the patrol car, West Point, the executive suite, the Judge's chambers and the football team. We have preached human rights and minority-group rights and non-discrimination, but we seldom give a job to a person whose age is above 65. The Universal Declaration of Human Rights adopted by the United Nations says in Article 25:

"Everyone has the right to a standard of living adequate for the health and well being of himself and his family including food, clothing, housing, medical care and necessary social services, and the right to security in the event of unemployment, sickness, disability, widowhood, old age . . ."

But there is nothing in these goals about retirement before old age, nor about Dr. Selye's heavily-emphasized dictum: "Man must *work*. Work is a *biological necessity.*"

Nor for that matter do they explain the *source* of the standard of living or of the security we are all apparently entitled to. Perhaps that is why the goals are unachieved in the great majority of countries.

When the "retired" people get all that political clout one reads about, it can be expected that they will get active about this whole area of access to creative, useful work, paced to suit them. Providing this less onerous work on a "phased retirement" basis would seem to be one of the social challenges that should lie ahead, and meeting it should prove to be much less difficult than many of the other challenges we have survived in recent decades.

As age advances, there are other needs. "The real test of a society is how it copes with its lonely people. In particular we must not forget or neglect the needs of the elderly, the handicapped, the social misfits . . ." That comes from the report of the Royal Commission on Social Security in New Zealand, 1972.

The one great service provided by pension plans, the regular arrival of the monthly pension cheque, does nothing to meet many of the problems of aging. Should not the field of those who provide these pensions be broadened, so that "pension planning" leads into a more comprehensive "social engineering"?

We have shown that housing expenditures do not decrease as age advances, and are the largest cost item in old age. Yet housing needs do shrink. Why is this? Is it not because every encouragement is given to remain in the same house, with all its memories, until long after its economic use has passed, and to leave it only when its costs and maintenance problems can simply no longer be coped with and it has itself become a burden of major proportions?

Does this not suggest the need for a greater number of smaller units built to be maintenance free, or serviced on an economical basis, separate to meet the psychological needs for independence and privacy, yet not isolated, so that neighbors are never far away and can be called upon in time of need? For those in need of regular visits from nurses, social workers, meal services, day-care centres and auxiliary services, a well-planned grouping of such residences could more efficiently meet both housing and other needs than the extremes of widely separated individual family homes lived in long beyond their time, or the dreaded dormitory life of the "home for the aged."

There are already two million people in Canada whose age is above 65, and every day 400 more people are entering that group. Life expectancies are increasing. We must recognize the place and special needs of these people.

Sadly, the life expectancy of males does not equal that of females. Too many of the elderly are women, many of them widows, living alone. Apart from the more outward problems of coping and survival, many are bearing the psychological burdens of stress, loneliness, loss of status, rejection, grief, denial of sex life, resentment, and even guilt. Not accustomed to dealing with the problems of mortgages, insurance, malfunctioning automobiles, leaking roofs, contracts, taxes and credit, they have needs that extend far beyond the pension cheque, and will sometimes call in the plumber not only to fix the faucet but because they long for masculine conversation.

Widows are a large and special group whose numbers are increasing. Not well recognized in many pension systems, they could well become the next group to be heard from in our social evolution.

At the end of the life in retirement comes death—a necessary part of life itself, and a time for respectful recognition both of the life completed and of the trauma and sudden extra costs faced by survivors. Here is another occasion in which the provision of regular pensions during life might be broadened to recognize this extra time of need that comes at the end.

In John Ciardi's translation of Dante's *Inferno* there are these lines:

"I am the way to a forsaken people
I am the way into eternal sorrow . . .
Abandon all hope ye who enter here."

May we so plan and build that no one will ever think that these would be fitting words graven over the Gateway to Retirement. Rather than abandon hope, we must continue to work usefully, to remain active and creative. We must have and provide companionship, mutual assistance, and full participation in society.

In Virgil's *Aeneid* we read how, as Aeneas approached the

162

river Styx, he found the shoreline crowded with "an airy crowd which filled the margin of the fatal flood . . . thick as the leaves in autumn strow the woods,

> "Such, and so thick, the shiv'ring army stands,
> And press for passage with extended hands."

In the world of the future, we must so plan that those who reach retirement age can in no way be compared to the shivering army described by Virgil, waiting "with hollow groans and feeble cries" at the edge of the Styx.

In a positive spirit, we must plan so that the later years will indeed be years of true self-realization, creativity, stimulation, development, growth and self-respect.

CHAPTER NINE

Conclusion

In this book we have seen how a great tidal wave of population is sweeping up through the age groups, and how this flood of people will reach pension age within the lifetime of most of us, changing the balance, and tending to double the ratio of pensioners to workers.

We have seen the dangers that lurk in the present movement toward an earlier average retirement age; this could cause the pensioner burden not to double, but to triple or quadruple in time.

We have seen how Canada's capacity to increase its productivity, to overcome inflation, to employ its surging work force now, and to provide pensions for them later depends in a crucial way on new capital formation, and we have seen that an important source of this capital is the growth of the reserves held by those pension funds that are actuarially funded. In general, these are the private pension funds. Many of the government-sponsored plans, such as the OAS/GIS, the C/QPP and the civil service plans are making either no contribution at all, or only a partial or temporary contribution, to the solution of these basic economic problems.

We have read the ominous message of rising taxation inherent in these non-funded, temporarily and insufficiently funded plans, and the serious threat that these rising taxes will pose to our Canadian way of life.

Turning our attention to inflation, we have noted the importance of ridding Canada of this scourge. To the extent that we fail in this, we have seen how to respond to this problem without overreacting or magnifying it.

With this ground covered, we have looked critically at the deep-seated funding and structural problems of the C/QPP and have noted the heavy damage to the Canadian economy and people which would follow from an expansion of that system.

We have indicated how the private funded pension plans, helpful as they are to the economy, must extend their coverage and their portability, and improve in other ways, and how a greater use of the rapidly rising RRSPs could help.

We have shown how government regulatory and tax policies, by removing present anomalies, could assist greatly in getting improvements made.

The funding of both the federal and provincial government pension plans for their own employees is a disaster area. Vast open-ended commitments have been made which will throw very heavy tax burdens on future generations of Canadians, but the tax-paying public who are expected, along with their children, to make good on these commitments, have not been informed. We have suggested that a proper investigation be made into this field, and policies established which will safeguard the future financial integrity both of the provinces and also of future generations of taxpayers and pensioners.

Finally, we have looked at retirement itself as a social institution, and have questioned the validity of a full cessation of work as a desirable end in itself to be imposed by mandatory elimination from the work force. Noting the enormous contributions made by those over age 65 in former times, even when expectations of life were much shorter than today, we have questioned the need to sacrifice the large potential economic input of those at the higher ages, at the cost both of heavy psychological damage to them and the increasingly heavy tax and other costs needed to sustain them in idleness.

A more gradual transition from full-time to part-time work and ultimate retirement seems indicated, and with it a basic redesign of our whole approach to the provision for and process of retirement, and a continuing concern for the changing needs of people as age advances after retirement.

If rising productivity permits an increase in leisure time, this would probably be best spread over the whole of an extended work life, not concentrated in a prolonged period of aimless idleness at the end. Nor is it the purpose of pension plans to provide a duplication of incomes during the period of full-time work.

Canada, to survive and meet its challenges and prosper, seems to need a change of emphasis toward a more savings-oriented society, with its future pension obligations more fully funded than at present, and with its resultant capital accumulations directed toward those applications which will most effectively:

—Increase productivity, hence overcome inflation.

—Provide jobs for the 18%-25% of the *young* people now unemployed.

—Position the economy and social outlook to meet the rising tide of pension costs now visible.

—Keep faith with the next generation, so that its tax burdens will not exceed ours.

It would seem that investment by the private sector offers better prospects of achieving these various goals simultaneously than does investment by the government sector.

To seek relief from the growing pensioner-to-worker ratio through expanded immigration would unfortunately result in accented pressure for capital, energy and resources. Canada needs extra capital more than it needs extra people.

Interwoven with this basic shift in emphasis to a more savings-oriented society are the strengthening of the funded pension systems, the improvement of their responsiveness to individual needs, and the problems of funding the public systems and investing their assets in a manner that truly strengthens the economic sinews of Canada.

Great challenges that seem to overshadow the future of nations—much as the vast pension-cost surge of the next century

166

now seems to overshadow Canada's future—can be dealt with successfully if they are perceived and understood in good time. The avoidance of large-scale errors of policy, during the time when necessary social adjustments are being worked out, is just as important as the development and implementation of the steps needed to overcome this threat that presently looms over Canada's future.

Also from Financial Post Books:

Takeover, by Philip Mathias, the inside story of a massive takeover: the 22 days of risk and decision that created the world's largest newsprint empire, Abitibi-Price.

The Risk Takers, by Alexander Ross, a lively study of real-life Canadian entrepreneurs and how they made their dreams come true.

Galt, U.S.A., by Robert L. Perry, an award-winning study of the "American presence" and foreign ownership in a small Canadian city, seen through the eyes of its people.

Women in Business, by James E. Bennett and Pierre M. Loewe, the first popular study of the dangers and implications of the shocking treatment of women in Canadian organizations.

Your Money: How to Make the Most of It
Your Guide to Investing for Bigger Profits
Life Insurance & The Businessman
Real Estate for Profit
Running Your Own Business
The Financial Post Investor's Handbook
The Financial Post Money Management Book

Financial Post Books
481 University Avenue
Toronto, Ontario
M5W 1A7